The Golf Doctor

The Golf Doctor

*How to Play a Better,
Healthier Round of Golf*

Bill Mallon, M.D., with Larry Dennis

Macmillan • USA

MACMILLAN

A Simon & Schuster Macmillan Company
1633 Broadway
New York, NY 10019

A catalogue record is available from the Library of Congress.

ISBN: 0-02-860853-4
Manufactured in the United States of America

10 9 8 7 6 5 4 3 2 1

*To my parents, John and Evelyn
Mallon, for all they've meant to my
life in golf and medicine.
And to Bill Strausbaugh, for all he
meant to my golf game.*

Introduction

I've known Bill Mallon for twenty years or so, before he was Dr. Bill Mallon, orthopaedic surgeon, and was simply a talented young golfer trying to make it on the PGA Tour. As an amateur growing up in the Northeast, he had been a phenom, and as a collegian at Duke University, he had been one of the best amateurs in the country. Then he played for four years on the PGA Tour, with some success. He didn't win a tournament, and he won't make the Hall of Fame, but to those of us in the business who watch and cover golf, simply reaching that highest level of competition is a wonderful achievement.

Bill left the tour to resume his studies at Duke and is now an orthopaedic surgeon with Triangle Orthopaedic Associates in Durham, North Carolina. He is now only an occasional golfer, although he hasn't lost his touch. On one of my visits to Durham, Bill and I were scheduled to play golf on a Sunday afternoon at his current club, Treyburn Country Club, which features a marvelous and difficult Tom Fazio course. It was mid-July, and he announced that this would be his first full round of the year. He had spent the previous two and a half days on emergency call, during which time he had performed about fifteen surgeries, and he was tired. So he made six birdies, including three in a row at one point, and finished with a one-under-par seventy-one.

Dr. Mallon is a prolific writer of medical papers and is the author of the "Ask the Doctor" column in *Golf Digest* magazine. He also is an Olympic Games historian and has published numerous books on that subject. A fitness buff, he practices what he preaches in this book. I spent a couple of hours with him one afternoon as he went from store to store loading his van with exercise equipment for the workout room he was building in his house.

In short, Dr. Mallon has all the credentials required to write a book about golf.

And I may have all the credentials—some I wish I didn't have—to be Bill's collaborator. I have written a dozen or so golf instruction books and countless instruction articles for *Golf Digest* and now *Senior Golfer* magazine. In doing that, I have learned that there are many ways to swing a golf club and strike a ball effectively, which is part of what this book is about. I've learned the same thing from personal experience because I've suffered from too many of the ailments discussed in these pages, starting with the usual bad back and progressing to arthritis in several joints. I've therefore had to learn a lot of different ways to swing the club along the way.

In the fall of 1993, Bill assisted his associate, Dr. Ralph Liebelt, in replacing both my knees with artificial joints. As this is being written, I'm scheduled to receive a hip joint replacement from Dr. Liebelt.

At the moment, my knees are the best parts of my body. The artificial joints have not interfered with my golf and, surprisingly, have helped it. I'm hoping for the same from the new hip joint. The point is, as Dr. Mallon tells us, there is always hope.

This book is more than just an exercise book, although it includes many exercises that improve strength and flexibility. It is chock full of common sense and methods that help us overcome or play around the ailments that we all have. We've also included advice that helps avoid injury and other dangers inherent in any outdoor activity.

There is, of course, no magic panacea here. Dr. Mallon warns that any exercise program or other treatment for injury or disease should have the approval of your physician or surgeon. He also advises, with a few caveats, that an occasional—or perhaps more than occasional—visit with your golf professional might not be a bad idea.

Given that, this book should improve the quality of your golf and your life.

Larry Dennis
Huntington, CN
October 1995

Author's Introduction

I've had the great fortune to have two wonderful careers. Since I graduated from medical school in 1984, I've been an orthopaedic surgeon, but the great dream and goal of my early life was to be a professional golfer. From 1975 through 1979, I achieved that goal and played on the PGA Tour.

Many people with medical problems play golf, and many golfers have multiple aches and pains or play with chronic diseases. I have the advantage of being able to look at this connection from the viewpoint of a doctor and a professional golfer.

In my two careers and life, I've gained the unique perspective of seeing three classes of golfers. In the mid-to-late 1970s, I was in my early twenties and one of the best-conditioned golfers on the tour—one of the early disciples of Gary Player's credo that playing your best golf requires one to be fit. Many of my peers were in similar condition.

Now I'm in my midforties, and I leave the house most days before the sun rises, and I usually get home after sunset. I have little time for golf and the exercise my body craves, and now I can sympathize with the golfers whose careers limit the time they have available to play this wonderful game.

Each day in my office, I see the third group of golfers. These are the older players, often in their sixties and seventies, who, now with the time to play the game they love, are often unable to play because of various ailments.

This book is not aimed at the twenty-four-year-old limberback who can do anything that's written in the monthly golf magazines. I can still pull off most of those acrobatics, but many of my patients can't. What's good for the touring pros isn't good for the fifty-year-old executive with limited time to play and exercise. In these pages, I'll try to address how golfers can play their best no matter what their ages or physical conditions.

Some of my ideas will be diametrically opposed to "classic" methods of golf teaching. It's not that I disagree with most of that teaching. In fact, I usually agree with it—if your goal is to play on the PGA Tour. The classic tenets of golf teaching are great for the touring pros. The tour pros, however, don't usually need this book. You do.

As always with any book, I have many people to thank. I always start with my parents, Jack and Evelyn Mallon, because they helped me get on the PGA Tour and through medical school, and my wife, Karen, because she has always willingly put up with these crazy lives I've led.

Several people helped me with a few sections of this book in areas outside my specialty of orthopaedics. My thanks go to Herb Stevens—"The Skiing Weatherman"— and Larry Nelson's old tour caddy who now earns his living as a meteorologist and who helped with the sections on lightning and weather. Dr. A. Elise Weinrich, Dr. Dwight D. Perry, and Dr. Charles B. Kahn helped with the sections on, respectively, skin problems, eye problems, and diabetes. Dr. Edward A. Palank of Manchester, New Hampshire, has helped with much of my understanding of the cardiovascular risks and benefits of golf. Dr. Deborah L. Squire, a medical sports specialist at Duke University, helped me a great deal with the section on women golfers.

And I'd like to mention Bill Strausbaugh, my former golf teacher and the professional emeritus at Columbia Country Club in Chevy Chase, Maryland. I never quite achieved as much on tour as Bill and I were hoping for, but perhaps with this book, I can repay him for his great help by making my own contribution to help other golfers.

Finally, I'd like to thank Larry Dennis. I've done a fair amount of writing now in the last few years, but I'm probably only about an eight from the whites. When it comes to writing about golf, Larry's a scratch from the blues.

Bill Mallon, M.D.
Durham, NC
October 1995

Contents

The Golf Doctor

1

What's at Risk?

Most weekend golfers bear little resemblance to the players who make their living on the professional tours. But the one thing the two have in common is they often sustain injuries or develop illnesses and still try to play despite these setbacks or illnesses.

Golf is the most popular participant sport in the United States. In addition, it's a lifetime sport, played by preschoolers and individuals well into their retirement years. The huge number of golfers and broad age-range of players guarantees that golfers who develop health problems, and there will be a high incidence, will have to contend with them if they wish to continue playing.

This book is the first attempt to look at the injuries and health problems unique to golfers. I'm an orthopaedic surgeon, but I'm also a former professional golfer who spent five years on the PGA Tour, so I'm familiar with both ends of the spectrum. In reading this book, you'll learn that you aren't the only golfer with a health problem. You'll also learn ways to continue to play golf and maybe even play better with your injuries and ailments.

Perhaps more important, we'll discuss ways to avoid these injuries, including exercise. The book, however, is not primarily an exercise book. Instead, the major emphasis is on ways to play around an injury. Many individuals have chronic back, shoulder, or other injuries that hinder their golf, but they would hate to give up the game they love. By focusing on the swing changes and on the playing and equipment modifications that can be made, you'll learn that you can continue playing despite a painful problem.

At the same time, proper exercise is important in helping you overcome the problem. Exercise can not only help to avoid injuries—and that's really the best way to handle all physical problems, isn't it?—but also help to rehabilitate them once they occur. As we look back at the last three or four decades of professional golf, we see that physical conditioning has had a major impact on the ability of the tour players to play regularly and more consistently at a higher level. The same can be true at any level if only we would exercise.

In the 1950s, professional golfers were not noted for their physical fitness or for their conditioning programs. Weight lifting was even considered taboo for golfers because it would make you muscle-bound and unable to swing a club. That's no longer the case. You just have to know the right way to lift weights.

Back then, only one golfer, Frank Stranahan, was known for his dedication to bodybuilding. Stranahan came from a rich family, the heir to the Champion Sparkplug fortune, and in the late 1940s during the early part of his golf career, he was one of the top amateur players in the world. Indeed, he won several professional tournaments as an amateur. He turned professional in 1951 and played for several years on the PGA Tour, winning several events. He lifted weights frequently and traveled with a set of barbells, much to the consternation of bellhops everywhere, who had to haul his luggage around.

The next golfer to emphasize physical fitness remains its most famous golfing devotee yet—Gary Player. Player began his professional career in the 1950s in South Africa and quickly realized that to achieve his goal of becoming the greatest player in the world, he needed to learn to hit the ball farther. Player, a small man, standing only five feet seven inches, has never weighed more than 150 pounds. He enlisted the aid of a former Mr. Universe, Roy Hilligenn, and began a bodybuilding program. Player gained about fifteen pounds of pure muscle and felt that he added as much as thirty yards to his drives. This ability enabled Player to win eight major championships, and he became one of only four men to win all four of golf's major titles.

I was also fairly small, at about five feet nine inches and 170 pounds. In college at Duke University, I began lifting weights based on Gary Player's program, and I also gained about thirty yards on my tee shots between my freshman and sophomore years in school. When I played on the tour, more and more players became interested in fitness and conditioning. Many of us ran together, and a few of us lifted weights.

Today, professional golfers exercise frequently and stay in excellent shape, for the most part. Among the current professionals, Keith Clearwater is regarded as the most avid fitness buff. But he is far from alone. In the early 1980s, the PGA Tour contracted with Centinela Hospital in Inglewood, California. The hospital provided a fitness trailer that follows the tour around the country. Several physical therapists work in the trailer. Many of the professionals use the therapists daily for short workouts or for treatments of injuries. All the pros now realize the importance of fitness and prompt treatment of injuries.

Similar trailers now follow the Senior PGA Tour and the LPGA Tour. As any of you older than fifty might imagine, the fitness trailer is one of the busiest spots at any senior tournament. Lee Trevino, who broke a year-long victory drought with a win at the Northville Long Island Classic in the summer of 1995, specifically credited the tour's therapists for helping him overcome a troublesome neck problem. But all the senior professionals realize that regular workouts and treatment for age-related ailments will prolong their playing careers. And it will prolong yours, no matter at what age you begin, and will improve the quality of your life, too!

2

Famous Golf Injuries

In bygone days, golf was considered a sport for old men, a benign activity equivalent to a walk in the park. Injuries were certainly not thought to be part of the process and until recently had received little attention. Many earlier reports in medical literature consisted primarily of unusual cases such as fractures of the small bones in the hand. Other than that, how could you hurt yourself swinging a golf club?

This approach was unfortunate because it's now well established that you can get hurt playing golf and that golfers play in spite of numerous ailments, some minor, some major, some golf-inflicted, and some not.

A golf swing involves a large trunk rotation and requires both shoulders to be moved through a wide range of motion at very high speeds. The swing creates stress on even the well-conditioned professionals with efficient swings. It has been estimated that more than 50 percent of tour professionals have sustained some injury that required them to stop playing competitively from three to ten weeks. Like the demands of all other professional sports, the demands placed on the tour golfer to remain competitive require the golfer to continually push the body to the edge of overuse. It's not unusual for professional golfers to hit more than three hundred full practice shots, putt for several hours, and then play a full round of golf daily, requiring up to ten hours of continuous activity.

Injuries to recreational or weekend golfers probably relate less to overuse than to poor swing, no warm-up, and poor exercise techniques. The innocuous appearance of the sport causes most weekend athletes to overlook the injury aspect. Yet injuries occur among amateur golfers. Most don't place the same demands as pros on their bodies while playing golf, yet those lesser demands are placed on bodies not as well suited to the task as those of the professionals. In addition, their swing techniques are less refined and efficient.

Over the last few years, several studies have examined the body areas that are most commonly injured in both professionals and amateurs, men and women. The back was the most commonly injured area among the men. The wrist was the most commonly injured area among the women. Wrist injuries among the women may be related to their lesser strength, which doesn't allow them to absorb the force of impact as well. The back was the second most common body area injured among the women. The elbow was the next for both.

Shoulder and wrist complaints among male golfers were about equal. In women, as stated, the wrist is frequently injured. Women also injure their shoulders, but not as often as the men do. As for shoulder problems, most occurred in older players and involved pain in the left shoulders of right-handed golfers.

What about the legs? Golfers have some problems with the hips, knees, and ankles, but less than you might think. For some reason, these areas have relatively rare golf-related injuries.

In all the studies that examined amateur golfers, low handicappers were found to sustain injuries most often. I suspect that the reason is related to the frequency of play, because there's no other obvious reason for injury.

The studies showed that 54 percent of the professionals and 45 percent of the amateurs considered their injuries chronic. On average, these injuries caused the golfers to lose five weeks of playing time.

The most common treatments prescribed for golfers are rest and physical therapy. Amateurs are treated with rest more often than professionals are, a fact that makes sense because the professionals play golf as a career.

We'll discuss all the injuries just mentioned in the various chapters on each body part. We'll be more specific about what's injured and why, how the injury can be treated medically, how it can be treated by making golf or swing modifications, and how it can be prevented or avoided.

First, let's do a quick overview of the problems and how they have affected careers.

Back Problems

As noted, golfers injure their backs more often than any other body part. Frank Beard, an eleven-time winner on the PGA Tour, once commented that virtually all professional golfers have had back problems at one time or another. This statement is not surprising because back injuries are the most frequent cause of disabling illness among young people in this country. In all studies of back injuries, certain risk factors are identified that increase the risk of somebody developing a back problem. Golf is always listed as one of the hobbies that place the player at risk. In fact, back injuries constitute up to 50 percent of all the injuries sustained by male golfers.

The reason for the injury is the twisting and turning required by the full golf swing. These movements strain the discs between the bones of the back and put them in danger of rupturing, or more technically, herniating. In addition, many times the disc will undergo more subtle injury in which it simply wears out, termed *degenerative disc disease.*

In the late 1980s, Jack Nicklaus, generally considered the greatest golfer ever, almost saw his career end because of back problems. He considered surgery but eventually overcame most of his problems by consulting with a physical trainer and embarking on a vigorous rehabilitation program.

Among today's great professionals, Seve Ballesteros, Lee Trevino, Fred Couples, Greg Norman, Tom Kite, Payne Stewart, Fuzzy Zoeller, Dan Pohl, Peter Jacobsen, and Tom Purtzer all have seen their careers interrupted, at least briefly, by back problems. Zoeller and Pohl had surgery for ruptured discs and still were able to return to their profession—difficult enough for an accountant but especially tough for a golfer. Trevino, who overcame two back surgeries in the late 1970s to again win on the PGA Tour and become the Senior Tour's all-time leading money winner, underwent fusion surgery on his neck in 1994, returning to win again on the Senior Tour.

Probably, the best player who has had the most back surgeries and continues to play well is George Archer. He has had several operations on his back, including two for ruptured disks. He eventually underwent a fusion of the vertebras in his lower back. Amazingly, despite all his hospital time, he continues to play regularly on the Senior Tour.

Elbow and Shoulder Injuries

As I said earlier, elbows rank second to backs on the list of golf injuries. Shoulder injuries are a close third. Many professionals have played despite elbow and shoulder injuries, although several have required surgery to correct their problems. In many other cases, the players have been able to overcome their injuries without surgery.

Of the many types of elbow injuries, the most common is tendinitis. If tendinitis occurs on the outside of the elbow, it's commonly, if anomalously, termed *tennis elbow,* whereas if it occurs on the inside of the elbow, it's usually termed *golfer's elbow.* This term is really inappropriate (and I've been unable to discover its source) because golfers develop pain on the outside of the elbow (tennis elbow) far more often than they develop golfer's elbow. Many players have fought this difficult-to-cure problem.

More significant elbow injuries were overcome by pro golfers Ed Furgol and Calvin Peete. As children, both had elbow fractures that left them unable to fully straighten their left elbows. Despite this, Furgol won the 1954 U.S. Open, and Peete became a top player on the PGA Tour in the 1980s, renowned as one of the straightest drivers in golf. Also, the unusual swing of Miller Barber, a star on both the regular and senior tours, is a result of a childhood arm injury.

Most golfers with shoulder pain note that the pain occurs at the top of the backswing, a transition point in the golf swing when the club is changing direction and the shoulder muscles are subjected to significant forces. This position is also the point of maximum elevation of the left arm, and the pain may be related to shoulder tendinitis or even mild arthritis of one of the shoulder joints. A few shoulder injuries will cause pain at impact or early in the follow-through, indicating an unstable shoulder that's trying to come out of joint.

The most famous shoulder problem on the PGA Tour probably belonged to Jerry Pate, a phenom who won the 1976 U.S. Open as a rookie on the PGA Tour (Jerry and I went through the Tour School together in 1975). Pate later won the Canadian Open that same year, and he also won the 1982 Players Championship to go along with five other victories on the tour. By then, however, he was already experiencing significant shoulder problems. One report has it that he initially injured his shoulder trying to hack his ball out of the ferociously tough ice plant at Cypress Point Golf Club during the Bing Crosby Tournament, and that's logical. As with wrists and elbows, any sudden shock to the shoulder joint can cause severe trauma.

Pate suffered from shoulder instability, a condition in which his shoulder joint would not stay centered during his swing, causing him pain when the ball would try to slip out of the socket. He eventually underwent surgery several times. Pate has since concentrated more on his careers as a television announcer and golf course designer, although he continues to play. But his shoulder problems cut short what once looked like a great professional career.

Jim Simons had problems similar to those of Jerry Pate's, and as a result, his once-promising career also suffered. Simons was a top amateur from Pennsylvania who attended Wake Forest and almost won the 1972 U.S. Open as an amateur. But once he got to the PGA Tour in 1974, although he won three times, he never played as well as expected, in part, because of his shoulder difficulties.

The rotator cuff is a structure well known to readers of the newspaper sports pages. Baseball pitchers and football quarterbacks seem to have almost endemic problems with this series of four tendons around the shoulder. Rotator cuff injuries occur in golfers but not as often as they do in tennis or in sports that involve throwing. But Lou Graham and Gil Morgan have had rotator cuff surgery, and both later returned to playing professional golf.

Hand and Wrist Problems

While hand and wrist injuries trail the elbow and shoulder as sources of problems among professional and amateur golfers alike, they seem to be on the rise among tour players.

Most wrist injuries are caused by a single traumatic event, often involving striking a tree root or rock. As the golf club nears impact, it may be traveling at a speed of more than one hundred miles an hour (even with irons); the sudden deceleration caused by an unexpected impact can impart a great deal of stress and subsequent injury to the wrist.

The most famous hand ailment in golf history probably was the one sustained by Ken Venturi. Venturi is now a well-known TV golf commentator, but in the late 1950s, he was considered the heir apparent to Ben Hogan as the greatest player in the world. But he developed multiple health problems, and the mantle went to Arnold Palmer. Venturi's career was in disarray when he stunned the golf world by winning the 1964 U.S. Open in intense heat. But shortly after that dramatic victory, Venturi's hands began to hurt. In 1965 at the Mayo Clinic, he underwent surgery on both wrists to help him overcome carpal tunnel syndrome. Although the surgery improved his situation, his hands never returned to normal, and Venturi was never again the same player.

Golfers also may sustain an unusual fracture of one of the small bones of the hands called the hook of the hamate. This injury is discussed in more depth in the chapter on hand and wrist injuries. This bone is almost never injured except in athletes who grip an implement and sustain repetitive impact stress to the hand and wrist—notably golfers, tennis players, and baseball players. One famous example of this fracture occurred in the great late New York Yankee Roger Maris.

The most notable golfer to fracture his hamate hook was John Cook, a top amateur who won the 1978 U.S. Amateur and then began a promising professional career. He played well for several years, but in the late 1980s, he experienced hand pain. Unfortunately, the problem went undiagnosed for several years. (It is, admittedly, a difficult diagnosis because in nongolfers, it's exceedingly rare.) Cook eventually underwent surgery for the fractured hand bone and later returned to the PGA Tour with great success. After his surgery, he won three tournaments and more than a million dollars in 1992 and almost won the British Open that year, finishing second to Nick Faldo.

Lee Trevino also had hand problems, and in late 1992, he underwent surgery on a torn ligament in his thumb. Despite this, he was able to return to his winning ways on the PGA Senior Tour, although he was later hampered by those disk problems in his neck.

Leg Injuries

Golfers don't have problems with their legs nearly as often as athletes in other sports. Also, golfers sustain injuries less often to their legs than to their upper extremities or back. Still, many professional and top amateur golfers have played despite significant knee, hip, and ankle injuries.

At the 1995 U.S. Senior Open, retired Air Force General Bob Hullender made the cut and played the last round with Arnold Palmer. This achievement was remarkable because Hullender was playing with bilateral artificial hip replacements. His right hip had been replaced in 1986, his left in 1992, just after he won the Texas Golf Association Senior Amateur Championship. In 1994, he won the World Senior Amateur and the U.S. Senior Challenge, plus the George L. Coleman Invitational at Seminole, Florida. He was a medalist in the U.S. Senior Amateur, losing in the finals, and he was rated the top senior amateur in the country by Golf Digest. In 1995, in addition to finishing tied for second low amateur in the U.S. Senior Open, he played in the U.S. Amateur, the U.S. Mid-Amateur, and the U.S. Senior Amateur. That's quite an achievement for anybody, let alone a fifty-eight-year-old with two artificial hip joints. He also won a driving contest at the Champions Cup in Houston that year with a 317-yard effort, proving that joint replacement may not affect your distance at all.

Hullender, who continues a regimen of exercises for mobility, flexibility, and strength, also walks whenever he plays. "I'd like to think that I can be an inspiration to others with osteoarthritis or any other ailment," he says. "I'd definitely recommend the surgery to others. I hope they can see what I did and do the same thing."

You may not be able to do the same, but Hullender's case proves that you can indeed play golf well after hip replacement surgery.

Both Julius Boros and Patty Berg, legendary professionals who are members of their respective Halls of Fame, eventually developed hip arthritis and underwent hip-replacement surgery. Top club professional Mike Krak, a former tour player, also continues to play regional senior events despite having had both hips replaced.

Playing golf with a knee replacement is more difficult, for several reasons, mostly relating to the design of knee implants. To my knowledge, no professional continues to play competitively with a knee replacement, although many people still play golf successfully after this operation.

But on the Senior PGA Tour, Charles Owens played for nearly a decade despite a fused knee. Owens had been a paratrooper at Fort Bragg in the early 1950s when he sustained a severe fracture to his right knee. Knee replacement surgery was not available in those days, and Owens eventually underwent knee fusion, in which the knee is surgically made completely stiff. Despite this handicap, Owens had a successful pro career and briefly played on the PGA Tour in the 1960s and early 1970s.

Special Health Problems

As an orthopaedic surgeon, I would naturally be most interested in the various orthopaedic problems that occur in golfers. But golfers have had many other health problems. Many of these have ended careers. Some professionals have heroically continued their golf careers despite their problems.

Arthritis

Arthritis affects many individuals. The disease has multiple forms, but the particularly devastating types are termed *inflammatory arthropathies*. Senior golfer Bob Murphy suffers from one of these types. Murphy was a top player on the PGA Tour in the 1960s and 1970s after winning the 1965 U.S. Amateur title. But he developed his health problems in the early 1980s and spent most of his time thereafter as a television golf commentator. Murphy was helped, however, by a new arthritis drug (methotrexate) that greatly improved his condition. He returned to play on the Senior Tour, where he has been highly successful.

Diabetes

Diabetes is a terrible disease that receives little attention in today's media. The disease affects children and teenagers as well as adults. It involves multiple organ systems and causes problems with the heart, the eyes, the kidneys, the nerves, and the circulation. Amazingly, several top professional players have had successful careers despite this debilitating disease. In the late 1970s and early 1980s on the PGA Tour, Mark Lye played successfully while battling diabetes. He was followed by Scott Verplank, who had won the 1985 Western Open as an amateur, the first PGA Tour victory by an amateur in thirty years. Verplank later won the 1984 U.S. Amateur title before turning professional. As a pro, Verplank has had mixed success due to health problems, despite the greatness forecast for him. The limited success has been due to health problems, but as of 1995, he appears to be overcoming his problems and is playing better.

Probably the best professional golfer today who must daily deal with the problems of being a diabetic is the popular LPGA player Michelle McGann. McGann went on the LPGA Tour shortly after high school and immediately impressed everybody with her length off the tee, her good looks, and her fashionable clothing. Great things were predicted for her, but she struggled for several years before finally breaking through in 1995 to win several tournaments on the tour. She also continues to be one of the longest drivers in women's professional golf.

Cancer and Other Disorders

Professionals with other health problems continue to play despite the problems. Paul Azinger's recent struggle with lymphoma is well known. Azinger's cancer was diagnosed in late 1993, and he didn't play for much of 1994 while receiving chemotherapy. But he returned to the PGA Tour in late 1994 and is now returning to his previous form. His story is reminiscent of Gene Littler, the smooth-swinging Californian who underwent cancer surgery in 1972 but returned to win five tournaments on the PGA Tour and eight more on the Senior Tour.

Al Geiberger and Tony Sills have played professionally despite suffering from inflammatory bowel disorders. This can be very debilitating, especially while playing in the heat, because of the loss of fluids. In the early 1980s, Geiberger recovered from this problem to win nine tournaments on the Senior Tour, where he is still one of the standouts. In 1953, Babe Didrikson, perhaps the greatest women's athlete ever, developed colon cancer and won the 1954 U.S. Women's Open despite playing with the handicap of a colostomy.

Lightning

Later, we'll talk in detail about lightning and how to avoid injuries from it. Unfortunately, not all professional tournaments have been immune to this problem. In 1991 at the U.S. Open at Hazeltine near Minneapolis, a spectator was killed by lightning, and later that year, another spectator was killed by lightning during the PGA Championship at Crooked Stick Golf Club near Indianapolis.

Professional golfers also have been injured by lightning. The most famous example occurred in 1975 at the Western Open at Butler National Golf Club outside Chicago. On Saturday during that tournament, lightning enveloped the course, and all the players, officials, and spectators were at great risk. Three professionals— Lee Trevino, Bobby Nichols, and Jerry Heard—were struck indirectly by lightning flashes, and all but Heard were hospitalized. Fortunately, no one was critically hurt. All three players, however, later developed back problems, which was possibly felt to be related to their lightning-inflicted injuries.

Substance Abuse

Golfers also have been known to have problems with substance abuse, most notably alcohol. The first famous example of alcoholism was Willie Anderson, the Scotsman who won the U.S. Open four times, three times consecutively in the first decade of the twentieth century. In 1910, only a few years later, Anderson died, and his death is considered to have been the result of his fondness for the bottle.

Frank Beard, a PGA Tour star in the late 1960s and early 1970s, had a near-brilliant career cut short by alcoholism. In 1975, Beard carried a three-stroke lead into the final round of the U.S. Open at Medinah, but he shot a seventy-eight and missed the playoff between John Mahaffey and Lou Graham by a stroke. Years later, after successfully undergoing alcohol abuse treatment, Beard admitted that he was drunk the night before the final round. He played for five years on the Senior Tour, winning one tournament, and now is a full-time ESPN golf commentator with his life in order.

Larry Mowry is another recovering alcoholic who competes successfully on the Senior Tour, winning five times between 1987 and 1989. He has had problems with his balance and his back since then but is back on track as a consistent money winner.

The most famous recent case of alcohol abuse is that of John Daly. Daly was the wunderkind who won the 1991 PGA Championship at Crooked Stick. An undisciplined—at least at the time—young man, who is the longest driver on the PGA Tour and hugely popular with the fans, Daly had been lucky to get into the tournament as the seventh alternate. But after winning that championship, his penchant for drinking and the problems caused by it surfaced publicly over the next couple of years. At one point, he was briefly suspended from the PGA Tour for his behavior, and he subsequently enrolled in an alcoholic abuse program.

In 1995 at St. Andrews in Scotland, Daly completed one of the greatest emotional comebacks ever seen in golf when he won the British Open in a playoff with Italy's Constantino Rocca. By that time, he had been dry for more than two years, and he seems on his way to a great career.

Today, rumors of drug abuse on the PGA Tour surface occasionally, but no case has been authenticated, probably because players who give in to drug or alcohol abuse simply cannot cut it in the professional game. Golf is too precise and demanding, physically and mentally, to be played successfully if your faculties are dulled.

That, incidentally, applies to playing golf at all levels. Just say no to drugs and use alcohol sparingly if you want to play your best.

The Emotional Aspect

In golf, your emotions on and off the course play a big part in your ability to do well. Controlling your emotions on the course is a subject to which many books and countless articles have been devoted, and I won't go into that here. Just keep in mind that carrying your worries about work, family, or any other aspect of your personal life onto the course can be just as debilitating as a physical ailment.

Perhaps the saddest story of emotions affecting a golfer is the tale of Young Tom Morris, told here because of its drama and possible impact on the history of golf. Young Tom was born in Scotland, the son of Old Tom Morris, one of the first great golfers, and a great architect. Young Tom won his first tournament in 1867, when only sixteen years old. Later that summer, Young Tom followed his father back to Prestwick for the 1867 British Open, his first. He played very well, shooting 175 for thirty-six holes and finishing fourth. Old Tom, meanwhile, won the tournament. No one knew it at that time, but it would be a while before someone other than Young Tom Morris would win the British Open.

In 1868, seventeen-year-old Young Tom Morris won his first British Open, shooting 157 at Prestwick and defeating Robert Andrew by two shots. He successfully defended his title in 1869, and in 1870, Young Tom elevated himself to a new level by winning his third consecutive British Open with a score of 149. This was still the age of the featherie ball, a leather sac stuffed with goose feathers, which traveled only two hundred yards when struck the firmest blow. Young Tom's score won by twelve strokes and broke his own tournament record by eight strokes.

In the early days of the British Open, the prize was a championship belt. The founders of the British Open had declared one could only keep the belt permanently by winning three titles in succession, a feat considered unthinkable. But in 1870, Young Tom Morris retired that belt. There was only one thing to do—cancel the championship. There was no British Open in 1871. But this didn't stop Young Tom—or the British Open. A new belt was procured, and in 1872, Young Tom won his fourth consecutive championship.

Old Tom Morris had been the first great golf champion, surpassing his mentor, Allan Robertson. But Old Tom knew who was the top player in the family. "I could cope wi' Allan myself," he once said, "but never wi' Tommy."

In 1873, Young Tom Morris fell in love. His game immediately returned to the ranks of the mortals, and the townsfolk of St. Andrews whispered that love was the cause. In 1873, he finished third in the British Open, and in 1874, he was runner-up. He didn't play in the 1875 British Open, having gotten married late in 1874 and being busy at the club.

In September of 1875, father and son Morris traveled to North Berwick to play a challenge match against Willie and Mungo Park, another father and son tandem.

Young Tom had wished to stay at home because his wife was pregnant with their first child, although she was not due for a time. Still, he played, and he and Old Tom handed the Parks a defeat on the last hole. As they left the last green, Young Tom was handed a telegram telling him that his wife was gravely ill.

The Morrises boarded a yacht for the trip home across the Firth of Forth. A second telegram arrived shortly before leaving, but Old Tom kept it from his son. When they arrived back in St. Andrews, as they walked toward the town, Old Tom had to tell his son that his young wife had gone into premature labor, and she and the baby had died.

The doctor attending Young Tom's wife was named Boyd. Dr. Boyd wrote, "I have seen many sorrowful things, but not many like that Saturday night." Young Tom was inconsolable. He retreated completely within himself and refused to play golf, although he was often seen taking long, solitary walks around the Old Course at night, usually wiping away tears as he walked.

Young Tom Morris was the greatest golfer of his time, and he was a perfectly healthy young man. But on Christmas day, 1875, three months after the death of his wife and child, at age twenty-four, he was found dead in his bed. The cause of death was listed as a broken heart.

Back then, medical science was not exactly at the level it is today, and there may have been another, underlying cause responsible for Young Tom's death. But we do know that emotional trauma can cause and further many health-related problems. It is hoped these aren't to the point in any of us where they will cause death. But if your golf game isn't up to snuff and there's no apparent physical reason, try to set your emotional problems aside—or preferably solve them—before you go out to play.

The Inspiration of Comebacks

We're all inspired by comeback stories, in and of themselves, and perhaps subconsciously, because they tell us that we too can overcome injury and illness to do what we once did well.

The sports world, in particular, abounds with comeback tales, undoubtedly because sports often produce injuries. Among the most famous comebacks by golfers are those of Ben Hogan and Ken Venturi. They thrilled us when they happened, and they will continue to thrill us through history.

In 1949, Ben Hogan, at thirty-six, was the greatest active golfer in the world. He had endured years of struggle and failure, plus a stretch in the Army during World War II that had kept him from competition. But he had taken time off in the late 1930s to remake his game, and it had paid off. He had been the leading money winner five times in the 1940s. In 1946, he had won the PGA Championship and twelve other tournaments. In 1947, he won seven tournaments. In 1948, he had won the U.S. Open, the PGA, and the Western Open—the only man ever to accomplish that troika—and seven other tournaments. He was dominating the tour in early 1949, winning two of the first four tournaments and losing the fourth in a playoff, and he was again leading the money list. But on February 2, 1949, two days after he had lost a playoff for the Phoenix Open title to Jimmy Demaret, Ben and his wife were traveling through west Texas when a Greyhound bus, coming down the wrong side of the highway, crashed into their car. Valerie Hogan sustained only minimal injuries, mainly because Ben threw his body across her when he realized the crash was imminent. That may also have saved his life. Nevertheless, Hogan was a mess, with fractures in the collarbone, pelvis, rib, and ankle, plus a bladder injury and massive contusions in his left leg that would later threaten his life. A blood clot that reached his lung could have killed him, and another possibly fatal clot in his leg was discovered. Hogan survived only by undergoing dangerous surgery to tie off the veins of his legs to prevent further clots from reaching his heart. He was lucky to have survived, but many thought he would never play again. Some were not certain he would ever be able to walk.

They didn't know Ben Hogan and his resolve. In January 1950, less than a year after the accident, Hogan returned to competitive golf at the Los Angeles Open and almost won, losing to Sam Snead in a play-off. Later that year, he won the U.S. Open at Merion, striking his famous one-iron shot to the seventy-second green to tie Lloyd Mangrum and George Fazio, then shooting sixty-nine on his battered legs to beat them both handily in the playoff. That began his greatest— if shortest—stretch of golf. In 1951, he won both the Masters and the U.S. Open. In 1953, he performed the yet-to-be-matched feat of winning the Masters, the U.S. Open, and the British Open in the same year. He didn't play in the PGA because of travel conflicts with the British Open, but he won two other tournaments in an abbreviated schedule and was named the PGA Player of the Year for the fourth time and the Male Professional Athlete of the Year.

In 1955, Hogan lost in his bid for a record fifth U.S. Open title, when he was tied by unknown Jack Fleck's seventy-second-hole birdie, then lost in the playoff.

Until 1960, when he was forty-eight, Hogan continued to regularly challenge in the major championships, but his health problems definitely shortened his career. He later developed difficulty walking because of the poor circulation in his legs from the operation that had saved his life. But he had made a comeback that perhaps stands unchallenged in sports annals.

As mentioned earlier, in the late 1950s, Ken Venturi was considered Hogan's heir apparent. As an amateur in 1956, he led the Masters through three rounds but shot an eighty on the last day to finish second to Jack Burke Jr. After turning professional, Venturi won ten PGA Tour events through 1960 and again finished second that year in the Masters to Arnold Palmer. But he developed back problems and simply lost his confidence and his golf game. From 1961 to 1963, he won almost no money. After winning only $3,848 in 1963, his career seemed over.

But in 1964, he began to regain some confidence, his game returned, and he began to slowly improve. The 1964 U.S. Open was held at Congressional Country Club in Bethesda, Maryland, outside Washington. That was still in the days when thirty-six holes were played on "Open Saturday." On that day, the temperature in Washington was more than one hundred degrees, and the humidity was extremely high. Venturi wasn't leading after Friday's second round, but on Saturday morning, he shot a sixty-six despite bogeying the last two holes of the third round. By then, the heat had begun to affect him, and he was trembling and lightheaded.

Between rounds, Venturi was attended by a doctor who advised him to withdraw. But he felt he was too close to a complete comeback to quit now. Accompanied by a doctor and a priest, he played the last eighteen holes almost in a daze. On the last hole, he turned to USGA Executive Director Joe Dey, apologized for walking so slowly, and told Dey to go ahead and penalize him (for slow play) if he had to. Dey replied, "Kenny, you're doing fine. Just hold your chin up proudly and keep walking. You're about to be the U.S. Open Champion."

On the last green, Venturi sank a fifteen footer for a par and then placed his hands on his head, exclaiming, "My God, I've won the Open." His playing partner was twenty-one-year-old Raymond Floyd, who took his ball out of the last hole and handed it to him. When Venturi saw his face, he began to cry, for Floyd was sobbing almost uncontrollably.

Late in 1964, Ken Venturi was named Sportsman of the Year by *Sports Illustrated* for his comeback victory and also for three other PGA Tour wins in that year. But soon after, he developed carpal tunnel problems in both wrists and never again played as well.

In that one short span, however, he—as did Hogan and many others—became an inspiration to us all.

So golf can be a tough game. But it's a great game, too. Come with us, and let's see how you can play it despite any aches or pains or other health problems you might have.

3

Equipment Modifications

Your golf equipment (usually) consists of fourteen golf clubs, golf balls, golf shoes, a golf bag, maybe a golf glove, and golf attire. You have many choices in all those categories, and those choices can have a definite bearing on how well you play the game and on your health. Golfers with certain injuries and ailments can make choices that may allow them to play better and also may ease the pain. In some cases, the old bromides about equipment and its effect on your body are probably not significant, and I'll point these out to you.

Your Golf Ball

In wound, or three-piece, golf balls, the force transmission is different from that of two-piece golf balls. The rumor is that using a wound ball will take stress off the wrist and elbow for players with injuries in those areas.

Wound balls consist first of a center, either solid or liquid, around which rubber filament has been wound tightly. Around the winding is a cover made of balata (a natural rubber from the balata tree, although almost all the balata used in golf balls these days is synthetic), Surlyn (a hard, durable thermoplastic), or blends of other thermoplastic and rubber materials that provide varying degrees of hardness, durability, spin, and feel.

Two-piece golf balls consist first of a rubber-type center that forms the bulk of the ball. The cover of two-piece balls is invariably Surlyn or one of the other blends. Any of the balls with these plasticlike covers will feel harder than one with a balata cover, whether it's natural or synthetic, and indeed, they are harder. This is especially true of the two-piece ball.

No scientific evidence exists, however, to back the claims that wound, balata-covered balls impart less shock to the wrist and elbow. Considering that in either case, the ball can legally weigh no more than 1.62 ounces and that it's being struck with an implement that weighs much more than that at speeds ranging up to one hundred miles an hour or more, the difference in hardness would seem insignificant in terms of force transmission. The shock of the clubhead striking the turf on iron shots is a hundred, maybe a thousand, times more traumatic. As I'll discuss later, the type of golf club shaft has much more to do with the transmission of shock to the hands and arms than does the type of ball.

From the standpoint of playability, there are significant differences between the two types of balls and the two types of covers. Two-piece balls have a larger moment of inertia than wound balls do because most of the weight of the wound ball is concentrated at the center, and more of the weight of the two-piece ball is in the cover—in other words, on the perimeter. The two-piece balls, therefore, will spin less than wound balls will. It's similar to the figure skaters who bring their arms close to their bodies to spin faster. If the weight is concentrated near the center, the ball will spin faster. Thus, wound balls will spin more and achieve more backspin on landing. Two-piece balls will have less backspin and will run more, especially with the longer clubs like the driver. They also have been found to fly higher and farther off the irons.

You should choose a ball that best matches your game. Higher handicappers will benefit from the increased distance they get from a two-piece ball. Lower handicappers usually like the feel of a wound ball, and they usually don't need the increased distance, although shorter hitters may. The professionals and better amateurs also prefer wound balls because of the spin they can impart, which helps their shots hold the green better.

Covers of Surlyn and other plasticlike materials are much harder to cut. The pros get their balls free, and they also don't hit that many bad shots, so cutting balls is not a problem with which they're concerned. The majority of amateurs tend to occasionally, if not often, mishit the ball. And golf balls are expensive. So if economy is a concern, you'll be better off with a ball that has a more durable cover.

One other ball characteristic that can help your game should be considered—the dimple pattern. Until about 1970, all golf balls had identical dimple patterns. The first ball to change was a strange bird called the Royal Plus 6, which had hexagonal dimples and flew incredibly high. In my first experience with this ball,

I hit a driver into the wind and watched the ball get blown nearly back at me. Soon other balls emerged with new and different dimple patterns. Most of them had a greater number of dimples (to this point, there had always been 336), were made deeper, and were arranged in different patterns. These made the ball fly higher, which presumably helped the average player.

The tour players, however, didn't like the new stuff. Most already hit the ball high enough. Titleist came out with a new ball with deeper dimples, and it flew way too high for the pros. Titleist lost a lot of its following among the tour pros, who switched to other brands. So the company produced a newer ball called the Low Trajectory Titleist. That still flew too high for the tour players, so next came the Pro Trajectory Titleist. This was what I used while I was on tour, but the joke among the players was that the next version would be called the No Trajectory Titleist.

Titleist recovered its popularity with the tour players, and the company eventually was proved to be right. Today, almost all balls come in varied dimple patterns that provide for various flight heights and trajectories and have different cover substances and interior designs that result in different feel and, to some extent, distance. Realistically, the difference in distance among the various brands is minuscule. No ball can go farther than the Overall Distance Standard established by the U.S. Golf Association in 1976, which means you should concentrate on the aspects of feel, trajectory, and durability that best suit your game. You can discuss these with your professional, who should be able to help you choose the best ball for your game. Choosing a ball that flies higher will benefit the higher handicapper who often has trouble getting the ball in the air and holding the ball on the green. This type will likely increase your distance and prevent you from artificially adjusting your swing to lift the ball in the air.

Your Clubs—The Shaft, the Clubhead, and the Grips

Now about those fourteen clubs in your bag. (The Rules of Golf limit you to no more than fourteen clubs in competition.) It was so much easier when I was playing the tour in the 1970s. Almost everybody used steel-shafted clubs with forged iron heads. We usually chose our clubs based on look and feel.

With the 1980s, however, came the technology explosion in golf. Now metal woods are the rage, along with hugely oversized clubheads on those "woods." Most irons are perimeter-weighted and cavity-backed. These features increase the effective hitting area, which allows a player to get better results from mishit shots. Graphite shafts, although they were available in the 1970s, now are much more consistent and have become popular with both amateurs and tour professionals. There are many other exotic materials now available for shafts, notably titanium and boron, along with mixtures of various other composites.

Many graphite shaft manufacturers state that their shafts are better for golfers with wrist and elbow problems. This has not yet been proven scientifically, but I suspect it's true. I'd recommend that any golfer with chronic wrist and elbow problems use graphite shafts if he or she can afford them (they are more expensive). The graphite has a softer feel and would seem to impart less shock to the wrist and elbow, thus decreasing the chance of injuring those areas.

I don't think the titanium and boron or other composite-type shafts will help as much as the graphite, although this also has not been proven. I would suspect that those shafts are better for your wrists and elbows than are steel shafts. They also are fairly expensive.

Brunswick, one of the world's major shaft manufacturers, has developed a steel shaft that tapers smoothly from top to bottom. The company claims that this shaft reduces the impact shock over the conventional steel shaft that narrows in steps.

H&B/Powerbilt, one of the old-line golf club manufacturers, has introduced a rubber appliance that fits into the shaft under the grip. The company says this appliance greatly reduces the shock to the golfer.

It's obvious then that shock and the possible injury to hands, wrists, and arms are considered a problem, and manufacturers are trying to do something about it.

Similarly, perimeter-weighted and cavity-backed irons should help all golfers with arm problems. When you hit the ball in the center of the club face, the type of clubhead you're swinging really doesn't matter. But on a mishit, the head will twist off center and impart a shock to your wrists and forearms. Perimeter weighting reduces the twisting, or torquing, on an off-center hit, lessening the shock to your arms as well as improving the quality of your shots.

As far as wood woods versus metal woods are concerned, I'm not sure it makes much difference in reducing injuries or lessening the damage in golfers who already are injured. The wood will have a softer feel and would theoretically seem to be better. But remember that metal woods can be designed (and are) to be perimeter-weighted and thus decrease shock transmission on off-center hits. Because of the shot and the swing with woods, there is little or no impact with the ground, especially when the ball is on a tee—well, unless you make a swing that I wouldn't wish on anybody.

In your grips, you have a choice of leather, materials that simulate leather, rubber, and cord-style grips. In addition, grips can be modified to be normal in diameter, oversized, or undersized. Leather grips have the softest feel and were the grip of choice through the 1950s. They are terrible in wet weather, however, unless they're kept perfectly dry. Rubber grips are better in the rain but can get fairly slippery in hot weather, when the hands get sweaty. Cord grips provide the best touch and grip in all conditions but are very tough on your hands. Many professionals use cord grips (I did), but they have developed thickened, callused palms that prevent skin problems on their hands.

Golfers with arthritis in their hands or wrists can benefit from oversized grips. The major grip manufacturers make "arthritis grips" that are significantly larger than normal and are also softer to help take the shock off the hands and wrists at impact. In addition, most pro shops sell grip tape that can be applied to further enlarge the grip. This material is tacky (which helps you hold the club more easily) and also fairly soft. Using grip tape may further help golfers with arthritic hands and wrists.

Undersized grips will benefit golfers without wrist or elbow problems but whose forearms and hands are fairly weak. The smaller grips allow the player to rotate the forearms faster through impact and to use the hands better to increase clubhead speed.

Special Clubs—Your Putter, Utility Woods, and Others

In addition to choosing the right shafts, clubheads, and grips, it may be important to determine which clubs you put in your bag.

For example, if you have back problems, the best thing you can do for your back while playing golf may be to put a longer putter in your bag. The worst thing anybody with a bad back can do is bend over for any length of time. Using a longer putter allows you to stand fairly upright and to take stress off your back, especially while practicing. The standard putter ranges in length from thirty-four inches to thirty-six inches. Ray Floyd, one of history's great players and great putters, uses a thirty-nine-inch putter, so he can stand more upright and practice longer in the conventional manner without tiring or injuring his back. You may even want to switch to the extra-long putter, one fifty inches or so. Longer putters require a different putting style, with the top hand holding the top of the putter snug to the chest and the bottom hand making the stroke. This method usually has been reserved for those with inherent putting problems—and it has saved several careers on the professional tours and considerable agony among amateurs—but it also requires you to stand more upright, thus easing strain on your back. In fact, in the early 1980s, the U.S. Golf Association was considering banning these extralong putters, but they demurred because many golfers and doctors noted that they were quite beneficial to those with chronic back injuries.

To that point, if your back hurts, consider making all your clubs longer than normal. Your golf shop or a local club maker can make this adjustment for you by changing your shafts. You can probably add one and a half to two inches without having to make major changes in your golf swing, and the added length will allow you to address the ball with a more erect posture.

Lower handicappers and pros usually carry a lot of long irons and only a few woods. Most touring pros carry only two woods—a driver and one fairway wood. This is not the case on the Senior Tour or the LPGA Tour, where many of the players carry several fairway woods, including one or two that are very lofted. The reason is strength.

Younger players on the PGA Tour have a lot of strength and can get the ball high in the air with long irons, notably a one iron, even out of bad lies. As you get older, however, you generate less clubhead speed and probably lose a little distance. Without the speed, it's harder to get the ball high in the air with the long irons. Female pros also don't generate the same clubhead speed as do the men (except perhaps for Laura Davies), so they have the same difficulty in hitting long irons high enough to hold the greens. This problem is even more accentuated for amateurs.

Unless you're very strong, you'll do better by forgoing the one and two irons and putting a couple of lofted fairway woods in your bag—perhaps a five wood and a seven wood. They're easier to hit, especially out of bad lies. Given this, you won't feel as though you need to go after the ball as hard to get it out of a bad lie. That easier swing will put your wrists and elbows at less risk of sustaining a major injury. And even the normal shots will pose less risk of damage to your body, simply because there is less impact shock with a wood than with an iron. Remember the words of Lee Trevino who once said that when lightning is in the area he holds his one iron over his head because "even God can't hit a 1-iron!" He was joking, of course, as we'll discuss later in a section on lightning. The real point is that most of us now hit better shots with fairway woods than with long irons—and with much less chance of injury.

What about swing trainers and heavy clubs? Should you have one? Should you use one? Can they injure you? I'll talk more about this in the chapter on exercises for golf. Basically, they may help a little bit. They are not a panacea and will not by themselves make you a better player, but they are unlikely to hurt you if you use them cautiously. The biggest problem with a heavy club or swing trainer is that it puts the shoulders at risk of rotator cuff strains, so be careful and swing it slowly. For warming up before the round, two or three clubs are just as good as the swing trainers.

Your Golf Shoes and Clothing

Golf shoes with metal spikes help by providing better traction, so you don't slip during your swing. They also help when walking on uneven ground by preventing you from slipping. The spikes make it a little harder for you to come up off your toes during your swing. Thus, some golfers with hip and knee problems, notably those with artificial hips or knees, may not wish to use golf shoes. It's a bit of a dilemma. Falling or twisting an arthritic or artificial knee is dangerous, so in that situation, golf spikes will help a lot. You'll have to make your choice based on your own experience on this one.

A compromise may be the new spikeless golf shoes. These provide a good grip, although a bit less than spikes. They also cause much less damage to the greens. Spikeless golf shoes may be the ideal choice for golfers with artificial or arthritic hips or knees.

Clothing is primarily a problem for golfers in very hot, very cold, or wet and rainy weather. I discuss much of this in detail in the chapter "Playing in Difficult Conditions." In the heat, wear light, cotton clothing, probably shorts (except for anybody with diabetes—see the chapter "Special Health Problems"), and use a wide-brimmed hat, sunglasses, and sunscreen. You also may want to use wristbands and perhaps even a headband to ward off the effects of perspiration on your hands and eyes. In cold weather, dress in multiple, thin layers rather than in a single, heavy sweater or jacket.

Your Bag, Your Cart, and Those Golf Cars

Now about your golf bag and how you get it around the course. Some of this advice may fall on deaf ears, but golf is a game made for walking. Walking the golf course is far and away the best way to play the game. Walking allows you to derive aerobic benefits and actually get some exercise from playing. Playing golf in a golf cart, termed *cartball* by former USGA president Sandy Tatum, gives the golfer little aerobic or exercise benefit.

You may demur on the grounds that you have health problems and need to use the golf cart. I would quote the words of Dr. Paul Dudley White, who is basically the founder of sports medicine in this country: "Before a person commits himself to a life of leisure with no exercise whatsoever, I would insist that that person have a thorough physical examination to be certain they are healthy enough to survive such a lifestyle." Translated, even if you have health problems, it's better to eschew the golf cart and walk the golf course.

Note that I neither request nor expect to ever receive any endorsements from any golf cart manufacturers. They hate me!

Ideally, if you can't or don't want to carry your bag, a caddie will be available for you. This is a wonderful way to play golf, although it's actually better exercise for the caddie than for you. Caddie programs have been declining for the last couple of decades, but recently, they've been making a bit of a comeback. Many clubs are making an effort to restore their programs. One prestigious club, Columbia County Club in suburban Washington, encourages caddie usage by levying a surcharge on cart riders. The surcharge is donated to the caddie program, helping pay any caddies on rainy days or simply on days they don't get out because of decreased play.

If a caddie isn't available or if you prefer not to pay for one, your alternatives are to carry your bag or to use a pull cart. Carrying your bag can be difficult for players with shoulder or back problems. You may be helped by the new bags that provide a double strap to go over both shoulders. This distributes the load better and takes stress off the shoulders and back. Pull carts are usually associated with public courses, but they make for a nice way to play golf, walk the course, and avoid straining your shoulders or back.

If you simply must use a golf cart for medical reasons, I emphasize one thing—be careful! Golf cart manufacturers prefer that we call them golf "cars," and in many respects, they're just that—an automotive vehicle. They don't go as fast as your family sedan, but they also don't provide you with the same protection. There are no seat belts or doors. You also don't drive the family car over the same type of terrain as you do a golf cart—or at least I hope you don't. There are very few cases of golf cart collisions, but there are many cases of golf cart accidents that have resulted in serious injury and even in death.

One of the best-known cases of golf cart injury involves Dennis Walters, a young club professional who several years ago crashed in a golf cart on a steep hill and was paralyzed from the waist down. A paraplegic for life, Walters has made a new life for himself as a famous trick-shot artist, operating, ironically enough, out of a specially built golf cart. He's a motivational force for physically challenged individuals everywhere, but I'm sure he wishes he had that last ride back.

As an orthopaedic surgeon, I've repaired legs that were hanging out of a golf cart and were shattered against bridge railings and the like. And lesser accidents happen commonly when a cart is driven carelessly.

So the rule is simple: Use common sense. Keep your feet and arms inside the confines of the cart. Be extremely careful when driving down steep hills, and never drive sideways on an incline. Carts tip easily, and it's also easy to fall out of one if you're not hanging on to something. Be especially careful on wet turf. A cart can slide out of control in a heartbeat.

So you have a lot of choices. You don't have to use the "standard" fourteen clubs, with standard shafts, grips, and heads, and you don't have to use a golf cart, with a big, giant tournament bag. Use the afore-mentioned guidelines, check with your professional on certain items, and make your own decisions about what's the best equipment for your own abilities and limitations to help you play better and to play around any injuries you may have—and to avoid others.

4

Exercises for Golf

There is a well-known golf story that concerns a player who asked his professional to teach him to swing like Sam Snead.

"No problem, Bud. But before we start, let me ask you to do a few things. Can you swing up one of your legs and kick the overhead door jamb for me?"

"Why, no, I don't think I can do that."

"Okay, Bud. Let's go out to the putting green. I'm gonna want you to lean over without bending your knees, and take a ball from the bottom of the cup."

"Look, pro, you know I can't do that. Look at this belly. Who do you think I am?"

"Sam Snead. He can do both of those things. Now when you can do them, come back and then I'll teach you to swing like Snead."

Get the point? Sam Snead has a superb golf swing and is one of the greatest players ever. But he was, and is, a tremendous physical specimen. Well into his sixties, he retained great flexibility and strength. The average player couldn't approach Snead's level of conditioning.

Golf seems like an easy sport physically, and I won't attempt to compare it with tennis or basketball in terms of physical demands. But playing professional golf, or good golf at any level, requires one to be in fairly good shape. Few of today's pros are in poor shape. If you want to improve your golf game, you need to get into good golfing shape.

The best way to improve your fitness level isn't to go to the local gym and ask the trainers what exercises to do. The strength coach at the local college isn't usually terribly helpful with the college golf team either. Golf isn't a sport that requires huge chest muscles or the ability to bench press one's body weight. Exercise regimens for golf should be very specific to the sport—as they should be for any sport.

Exercises to Help You Play Better

The best exercise to make you a better golfer is to play golf—and play lots of it. That may sound obvious, but it's true. One of the rules of athletic training is the specificity principle. The best exercise for any sport is the most specific one to that sport—play your sport and play it a lot.

In addition to playing, however, you can prepare to play better by building up specific muscles that help to prevent injury and develop a stronger, more efficient golf swing.

The most important muscles involved in the golf swing are those of the back, legs, forearms, and stomach (the abdominals). Developing the muscles of the chest, frontal shoulders (anterior deltoids), and biceps can hinder the swing, actually making it more difficult to make a backswing.

It's important to develop the lower back muscles and the abdominals. As I've mentioned, the back is the most commonly injured body part among golfers. The spine is similar to a tall radio tower supported by a series of four guy wires. The spine is supported by four sets of muscles: the back muscles, the abdominal muscles, and the muscles along each side, termed the *obliques*. If any of these muscles become weak, which often happens to the abdominals, excess stress is then assumed by the other muscles, usually those in the lower back. The lower back muscles occasionally cannot support the load and simply give out.

Thus, to support the lower back, keep the abdominal muscles strong. The best exercise for strengthening the abdominal muscles is termed a *crunch* by bodybuilders. It's actually an abdominal curl, in which,

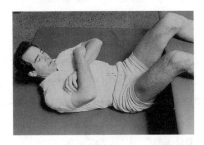 

Figure 4–1
Crunch or abdominal curl—
starting position.

Figure 4–2
Crunch or abdominal curl—
finishing position.

Bill Mallon Collection/Courtesy Mr. Sonny Falcone

*Figure 4–3
Trunk twist
with barbell.*

Bill Mallon Collection/
Courtesy Ms. Billee
Bullett

*Figure 4–4
Lateral or side
bends with
barbell.*

Bill Mallon Collection/
Courtesy Ms. Billee
Bullett

rather than doing a full sit-up, only the head and shoulders are curled up off the floor while the small of the back is kept pressed firmly against the floor. This movement should be done with the feet elevated and not held down, with the hip and knees flexed, and with the arms folded across the chest, rather than behind the neck. The beginning and ending movements are shown in Figures 4–1 and 4–2. This exercise isolates the abdominal muscles while decreasing the use of the hip flexors. Overusing the hip flexors can lead to

Bill Mallon Collection/
Courtesy Ms. Billee
Bullett

*Figure 4–5
A simple
exercise for
loosening up
your back.*

further back problems by increasing what is called lumbar lordosis, or a swaybacked appearance in the lower back.

Developing more back flexibility will also help prevent back injuries. Again, think of the radio tower. If any of the guy wires are too tight, when the wind blows or any stress is put on the tower, the tight wire may snap. This principle holds true for the back. Most people actually have fairly tight back muscles because they have been overstressed due to weak abdominal muscles.

Stretching the back primarily involves developing better trunk rotation, which is probably the key element in any flexibility program for golf. Two excellent exercises for back stretching are illustrated in Figures 4–3 and 4–4. Both involve placing a bar of some type over the shoulders. Both exercises are performed in the seated position. In Figure 4–3, the trunk is slowly rotated side to side. In Figure 4–4, the trunk is tilted toward the floor, and then, after returning to the upright position, the body is tilted toward the opposite side. Although the exercise can be performed with a broomstick or a golf club, a lightly weighted bar or stick, such as a barbell, will add a slight stretch at the end of the exercise, because the weight will pull the body through the last few degrees of stretch. This movement should be done very slowly to avoid injury. These two exercises are great because they not only develop flexibility, but also help strengthen the oblique muscles.

To increase flexibility, there are other important exercises to warm up and loosen up the back. These are similar to back-stretching exercises with which you're probably familiar. One is simply to sit in a chair and bend your head toward your feet (see Figure 4–5). This movement will loosen the back, but because your knees are flexed in the sitting position, it will not overstress the area.

Next is the *hurdler's stretch* (see Figure 4–6). This exercise is harder and should be done only after the first stretch in the chair or bench and after warming up. A variation of this exercise that is easier to do around golf courses involves placing one leg up on a rail or a

Figure 4–6
The hurdler's
stretch.

Bill Mallon
Collection/Courtesy
Ms. Billee Bullett

Figure 4–7
A variant of the
hurdler's stretch
that can be
done at the
course.

Courtesy Jim Moriarty/
Mr. Ed Ibarguen

bench and leaning over toward your feet. Do it slowly and gradually to avoid injury (see Figure 4–7).

Perhaps the ultimate exercise for developing flexibility in golfers is to swing a weighted club. You should try to maintain fairly good form by not letting the left heel rise too high off the ground on the backswing, by not rolling the weight to the outside of the right foot, and by keeping the left arm fairly straight. If these parameters are maintained, the stretch will be felt

*Figure 4–8
Squeezing a
rubber ball or a
tennis ball will
build up your
forearms.*

Courtesy Jim Moriarty/
Mr. Ed Ibarguen

entirely in the trunk and shoulders, and flexibility will be developed in these areas.

Once again, be aware that stretching exercises should be done slowly, so the stretch at the end of the movement is a gentle one. Otherwise, injuries can result.

The hands grip the club, and the forearms support and swing it, so strong forearms and hands enable you

*Figure 4–9
Wrist curl—
finishing
position.*

Bill Mallon Collection/
Courtesy Ms. Billee
Bullett

to maintain a firm hold throughout the swing without squeezing the sawdust out of the handle. In addition, developing these muscles provides some protection against wrist and elbow problems. Forearms are best exercised by simple repetitive compressive exercises, notably by squeezing a rubber ball or tennis ball. In a different sport, this was the method used by Rod Laver to develop a strong left forearm that helped him play tennis at championship levels (see Figure 4–8).

Also, various hand-and-wrist exercisers are available, although they're usually more expensive than a tennis ball or a rubber ball. Still, you may wish to try one. The nice part about building up the forearms is it can be done almost anywhere. If you're a businessperson, keep the exerciser or tennis ball on your desk and do some repetitive squeezing while on the phone. If you're a salesperson and on the road a lot, do this exercise while driving.

Three weight exercises that can develop the forearm muscles are shown in Figures 4–9 through 4–13. These are the wrist curl, the reverse wrist curl, and the wrist roller. In the first two, the barbell is lowered to the end of the fingertips, and then the fingers curl the weight back into the palm, followed by the wrists curling up to lift the weight another inch or two higher. The wrist curl is performed with the forearms supinated, or turned up, whereas the reverse wrist curl is done with the forearms pronated, or turned down. The wrist roller is performed by rolling the weight all the way up until the rope is fully wound around the bar (see Figures 4–12 and 4–13).

Figure 4–10
Reverse wrist curl—
starting position.

Figure 4–11
Reverse wrist curl—
finishing position.

Bill Mallon Collection/Courtesy Mr. Sonny Falcone

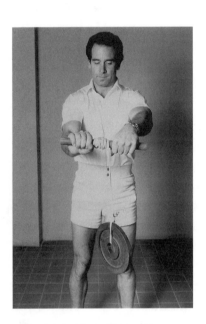

Figure 4–12
Wrist roller—starting the
weight down low.

Figure 4–13
Wrist roller—and rolling it
to the top.

Bill Mallon Collection/Courtesy Mr. Sonny Falcone

To be able to play better, you need good wheels—your legs have to be in shape. The best exercise for conditioning the legs is walking—walk the golf course. As I said earlier, it makes golf a better game, allows for better camaraderie with your playing companions, and makes the sport good exercise. As Shivas Irons said in Michael Murphy's wonderful book, *Golf in the Kingdom,* "Ye're makin' a great mistake if ye think the gemme is meant for the shots. The gemme is meant for walkin' . . . for if ye can enjoy the walkin', ye can probably enjoy the other times in yer life when ye're in between. And that's most o' the time; wouldn't ye say?"

If you're really interested in building up your legs for golf, you probably should start running or riding a bike. Either one is excellent for building up leg strength and for aerobic fitness. Running is more stressful on your feet, ankles, and knees, and injuries to those areas may preclude it. Cycling is more dangerous if you aren't used to doing it anymore, but if you are careful, it's actually easier on your joints. And if you don't want to worry about traffic on the roads, there's always the stationary bike. It's boring, but park it in front of a television set, and pedal to your heart's content . . . and I mean that literally!

If you have only a few minutes a day and wish to build up your legs, one excellent exercise is the wall sit. Position your back firmly against a wall and place your feet about one and a half to two feet away from the wall. Lower your buttocks until your thighs are parallel to the floor. Then hold that position for as long as you can—one to two minutes is very good. You will feel the burn in your thigh muscles. Skiers do this exercise a lot. Another advantage of this exercise is it can be done during the week at work in just a few minutes.

Nautilus machines at your health club or spa can help, but be careful. For the uninitiated, Nautilus machines are mechanisms that allow you to weight train without using barbells and changing plates. The machines are safer than using free weights and offer the theoretical advantage of exercising the muscles through a wider range of motion. As a result, they can increase flexibility as well as strength. However, free weights, when used properly, also help increase flexibility. The problem with Nautilus machines is they are not specifically designed for golfers, and some machines will develop the chest and frontal shoulder muscles more than you want and to the detriment of your swing.

On the other hand, several Nautilus machines exist that can be used to exercise the back, legs, and stomach. The stomach muscles are exercised by the abdominal machine. Strengthening these helps protect the lower back from injury. The legs can be exercised by using the Nautilus leg extension, leg curl, and leg press machines. The back can be exercised with the pull down machine and the reverse fly machine. All these are available at most clubs that feature a full complement of Nautilus machines.

Using the Nautilus machines properly can develop and tone the muscles that help your golf swing.

If you live in the northern half of the United States or anywhere else in the world where winter keeps you off the course for four or five months or more, you should be concerned about staying in shape to be able to play your best when the courses finally reopen in the spring. I know, the urge is strong to remain mired deep in that easy chair, your favorite drink in one hand, the channel changer in the other, while the snow falls outside. And then in a few months, after you lose all your bets to the players you usually beat easily, you'll wonder what went wrong. Wintertime may preclude your playing golf outdoors, but it doesn't keep you from helping your game while indoors. And it doesn't have to take hours.

Do some of the simple back stretching exercises that we've discussed. They can be done easily in your living room. Use a broomstick or a golf club held over your shoulder to work on trunk rotations and lateral side bends.

The best exercise you can do for golf is to swing a golf club. It doesn't take a rocket scientist to figure that out. But it's sometimes difficult to do this indoors in the wintertime. If your club sets up a net indoors or there's a nearby indoor practice facility, use it several days a week in the winter to keep your swing tuned up.

If neither is available and the ceilings in your home are too low, you can still swing indoors. I use a steel pipe filled with lead and covered by a golf grip. Although it's short, it swings like a slightly heavier-than-normal club, and that will also help your flexibility. The one I use is two feet long and has a heavy end and a light end. You can make one of these or order one of several available models from your professional.

It's important during the winter to keep your legs in shape. Come April, walking that course will require you to cover about five miles in about four hours. Those first few rounds will cause some soreness if you've completely neglected your aerobic conditioning over the winter.

You can do many different exercises at home to condition your heart, lungs, and leg muscles. The least expensive exercise, and an excellent one, is to run in place for about fifteen minutes—during halftime, of course. Other options, probably a bit more interesting, are a rowing machine, an exercise bicycle, a treadmill, a stair-climbing machine, or a cross-country ski simulator. These options are more expensive, but all are available in home models. Fifteen minutes a day on these will pay dividends when spring breaks.

Adding up the time to do three stretching exercises, swing a heavy club, and run in place for fifteen minutes (or a similar aerobic exercise), you can really help your golf game this winter in only thirty minutes of exercise done a few times a week. It's not really that difficult—just fifteen minutes during the halftime of the Duke-Carolina game, then fifteen more minutes after you've been inspired by *American Gladiators.* Go for it!

Golf as an Exercise to Keep You in Shape

Can you stay in shape simply by playing golf? Yes, you can, although you must walk the golf course. A golf cart is simply not an acceptable method for playing golf if you wish to derive some exercise benefit from it. Studies have shown that walking a golf course gives a player a significant aerobic workout. These same studies have shown that walking eighteen holes of golf several times a week will also help control high blood pressure and lower cholesterol levels. To see why this is so, let's examine how many calories are burned by walking a course over eighteen holes.

The best estimate for how many calories are burned can be made by simply using standard formulae for the number of calories burned while walking or running. The magic number is about one hundred calories per mile. The speed of walking or running has little effect on this number. Although it would seem that you would burn more calories if you ran faster, remember, the mile is then finished faster; therefore, you're not burning excess calories for as long. Although there are some minor variances, one hundred calories per mile is a reasonable estimate.

Most golf courses are about four miles long (7,040 yards = four miles). When you include walking to your ball, walking around the greens, and walking from the green to the next tee, most people probably walk about five or six miles while playing a full eighteen-hole round of golf. This amount of walking would burn about five hundred to six hundred calories. Carrying your golf bag probably adds a few calories, perhaps fifty to one hundred. Thus, by walking eighteen holes, you can burn about six hundred to seven hundred calories.

It may be true that golf isn't a major aerobic activity that raises the heart rate to high levels. This benefit for the cardiovascular system is usually considered one of the main criteria derived from aerobic training. Walking a golf course and playing golf raises the heart rate (especially when you're facing a three-foot putt to win the hole) but usually not high enough to be considered helpful. But again, studies have shown that it can help. Again, the reason is that the activity usually

Figure 4–14 Walking the golf course— the best exercise and the most enjoyable way to play golf.

Courtesy Jim Moriarity/ Mr. Ed Ibarguen and Ms. Jaime Koizumi

takes place over three to four hours and encompasses walking five or six miles.

So get out of that golf cart and walk that golf course. Enjoy the game more and get healthier at the same time. What more could you want? (see Figure 4–14)

Exercises for Hitting the Ball Farther

The distance a ball travels depends on many causes, but if the swing mechanics don't change, increasing club head speed at impact will always increase the distance the ball travels. Many good players feel that length comes from the legs, but it's necessary that the arms swing at a very high velocity to generate club head speed. The muscles of the upper back help swing the arms, especially the left arm, through impact.

Many professionals think that the best way to develop more club head speed is to swing a heavy club, so the regular club then will feel lighter and can be swung faster. But consider that most golf clubs are not terribly heavy—the heaviest iron would weigh fifteen or sixteen ounces, and the driver, which is the club that produces the most distance, is the lightest club in your bag. Strength is rarely the limiting factor in the ability to generate club head speed. What limits people, as odd as this may sound, is their ability to swing the club quickly.

Developing the ability to swing the arms more quickly increases club head speed and imparts greater velocity to the ball at impact. By swinging faster than maximum speeds, it should be possible to train the muscle fibers responsible for high-speed movement of the golf club. Although you may question whether it's possible to swing at faster than maximum, it indeed can be done by swinging a lighter club.

This principle is used by the Eastern Europeans—the former Soviet and East Germans, for example—in field events such as the shot put or javelin throw. Rather than train with heavier shots or javelins, they train with lightweight shots and javelins to increase arm speed, trying to develop the "quick arm." A similar method is used to train sprinters who are also faced with the difficult problem of finding a way to train at supramaximal speeds. Training is accomplished by either running downhill or being towed behind a motorcycle, which decreases wind resistance and pulls the runner just above his maximum for short bursts.

An excellent drill to increase arm and club head speed is to turn the club upside down and, holding the shaft just above the head, swing the club back slowly, and then attempt to make the loudest "whoosh" possible on the forward swing. It's possible to use a relatively normal club and still perform a similar drill. By removing the sole plate of a driver and taking all the lead out of the club, a very lightweight club can be created, weighing less than a C-0 swingweight. Swinging this club ten to twenty times a day will develop increased arm speed.

It should be cautioned that supramaximal velocity training is a very strenuous exercise, much more so than simply swinging a heavy club. It probably should be attempted only by tournament players or young players in fairly good condition. It shouldn't be attempted until you have fully warmed up by swinging a regular club or a heavy club at normal speeds for five to ten minutes. If you attempt these exercises, you'll be astonished at the amount of muscle soreness you'll feel the next day, so begin cautiously with only two or three repetitions of each. And if you have any ailments, which is probably why you're reading this book in the first place, don't do any high-speed training until you check with your physician or orthopaedic surgeon and explain exactly what you want to do.

In this discussion of training to increase speed and strength in the golf swing, it may seem that I've overlooked weight training. As I mentioned earlier, this has been popularized by Gary Player and is a valuable adjunct to any complete golf-training program. Unfortunately, most people who want to begin weight training for golf get their advice from bodybuilders or weight lifters who have little conception of the muscles used in a golf swing. Consequently, the program often includes a lot of bench presses or other exercises that aren't helpful to the golf swing and may even be detrimental. But, yes, a properly designed weight-training program should be able to help your golf game. I've discussed some of these techniques earlier in the sections on injury prevention.

As I've explained, club head speed is determined largely by how quickly the arms are swung going forward. For right-handed golfers, the arms are led by the left arm. Thus, the speed with which the left arm is swung will largely determine the distance one can hit a golf ball. If the golfer cannot swing the left arm quickly, it will become the rate-limiting factor, and the entire swing will slow down.

The left arm is swung across the chest by the muscles of the upper back. Two standard exercises to help develop lat muscles are chin-ups and lat pull downs (see Figure 4–15; lat is short for latissimus dorsi, the large muscle of the upper back that assists the left-arm swing).

Two exercises that are very specific to the golf swing are shown in Figures 4–16 to 4–19. The first exercise (Figures 4–16 and 4–17) requires access to pulley weights.

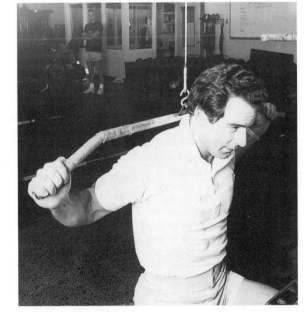

Figure 4–15 Lat pull downs—another exercise to build up the muscles that swing your arms.

Bill Mallon Collection/ Courtesy Mr. Sonny Falcone

Figure 4–16
Using weight pulleys to
build up your golf muscles—
starting position.

Figure 4–17
Using weight pulleys to
build up your golf muscles—
finishing position.

Bill Mallon Collection/Courtesy Ms. Billee Bullett

The player holds the pulley rope attachment in a position similar to that reached at the top of the backswing. Both arms are then swung across the chest, pulling down on the pulley. In the second exercise (Figures 4–18 and 4–19), the player leans over with a dumbbell in the left arm and swings forward from that position, imitating the golf swing from impact through the follow-through.

Warm-Up Exercises to Prevent Injury

Warming up before playing a round of golf is advocated by all golf professionals. Tour professionals always

Figure 4–18
Using dumbbells to build up your golf muscles—starting position.

Figure 4–19
Using dumbbells to build up your golf muscles—finishing position.

Bill Mallon Collection/Courtesy Mr. Sonny Falcone

warm up by practicing for at least thirty minutes before playing. No studies have shown any detrimental effects from warming up before participating in any sport, including golf. Thus, although specific studies haven't been done, it's likely that a short warm-up period before playing may benefit the performance of any golfer and possibly decrease the risk of injury. Yet a large number of recreational golfers rarely practice any full shots before playing a round. If they warm up at all, they often strike only a few putts on the putting green. That's the lowest-intensity golf shot and hardly prepares the player for a high-intensity effort on the first full drive. In some cases, the golfer's failure to practice before playing is due to the lack of adequate practice facilities. It is, however, in that case, possible to warm up with some stretching and swinging exercises.

Typical warm-up regimens begin with the player hitting golf balls on the practice range. A typical basket of practice balls contains about fifty balls, and these can usually be hit in about thirty minutes. Most professionals recommend beginning with short pitch shots played with a lofted club such as a wedge. These require only a short, low-intensity swing. After you hit a few of these, you then should gradually increase the length and intensity of the swing. After you have graduated to a full swing with a lofted club, you then can use the less-lofted clubs that hit the ball farther, eventually building up to hitting the last few shots with a driver. As the clubs decrease in loft, the length of swing and the length of the shot increase, and the intensity of effort increases commensurately. Thus, the longest shots should be hit only after fully warming up with less-lofted clubs.

After warming up by hitting full shots and before beginning actual play is the time to hit some short chips and putts on the putting green. Though it's unlikely that practicing putting and chipping will help you avoid injuries, it's quite possible that it will improve your performance when the round starts.

Some physiologists have stated that the routine I've just described does not constitute a proper warm-up. They consider a warm-up to be an activity that gradually takes the body from a state of rest to an optimal working condition. They recommend beginning with activities that increase body temperature, such as walking or slow jogging, followed by low-level calisthenics, stretching exercises, and then specific golf-related activity such as hitting golf balls.

This approach is ideal and cannot be faulted. Similar methods are often used by many professionals, but the recreational player can rarely afford the time to perform such a lengthy warm-up. It's likely that beginning with short shots and increasing the length and intensity of the swing, as described earlier, will gradually raise the temperature of the golf-related muscles and result in an adequate warm-up.

Swing Modifications to Help Hit the Ball Farther

One of the causes of sports injuries is usually considered to be poor technique. This idea has never been scientifically verified, and it may never be, but evidence can be deduced indirectly.

Studies have shown that professionals use a much lower percentage of their maximum muscular output potential during their swing than do most recreational golfers. Their efforts are less despite the fact that professionals tend to generate a higher velocity of movement in their body segments and consequently produce more club head speed.

It's likely that this efficiency is a result of the professional's use of a more refined technique. As the pro is using a lower percentage of muscular potential, he or she will likely avoid the high stresses often associated with acute muscle or tendon strains. Less stress doesn't, however, protect professionals from chronic overuse injuries that may be the results of the high frequency of practice and play they must undergo to be successful.

In golf, development of proper technique can be done by several methods. There are many golf journals and magazines that discuss techniques. In addition, many golf professionals have written books on learning to play with proper swing mechanics.

The golf professional at most courses or clubs is usually available for golf lessons to instruct the less-skilled player in the development of techniques that may make the player less susceptible to injury. In fact, if the player has a preexisting injury or injury tendency, the professional may be able to help the golfer design a swing that avoids stressing the affected body part. If a golfer truly wishes to spend the time to develop the proper technique to improve his performance and to decrease the risk of injury, lessons from a golf professional are most likely the best method to achieve this.

So you want to swing like Sam Snead? Well, get in shape, stay in shape, and get out of that golf cart. Warm up before playing, do some exercises at work or at home during the week, and exercise during the winter to get your body ready for the spring's first round. Take some lessons and discuss any health problems you have with your golf professional.

You can get stronger and healthier by playing golf—and you'll enjoy the game more and probably hit the ball a lot farther with a lot less effort. Keep at it!

5

Oh, My Aching Back!

If your back hurts while playing golf—or at any other time, for that matter—take comfort in knowing you're not alone. As I said earlier, the back is by far the most commonly injured body part among golfers. In fact, studies of people with back pain usually list golf as a risk factor in developing that pain.

There are many reasons people develop back pain. The back is a complex structure, and to understand the causes of your back pain, it's helpful to know something about human anatomy.

The back is made up of the spine, or the bones in the back, the spinal cord and nerves, discs, and the soft tissues. The bones consist of the vertebrae, which are stacked one on top of the other, similar to building blocks. Through the middle of each vertebra runs the spinal cord, from which nerves exit the bones to supply the muscles of the hips, buttocks, and legs. Between each two vertebrae lies a disc. The disc is the source of much pathology in the back. It's made of a fibrous, or gritty, material surrounding a jellylike center. The disc acts as a shock absorber in the back. The soft tissues surround the bones and nerves and include the muscles, the tendons, and the ligaments.

First, it should be remembered that not all back pain comes from the bones, nerves, discs, and soft tissues of the back. Back pain can be caused by many serious systemic illnesses. Notably, back pain can be caused by kidney disease, especially an infection, by gall bladder disease, by heart disease, and by an aneurysm, a balloonlike swelling of the body's major artery, in your abdomen. Several of these problems can be life-threatening, so anyone with long-standing back pain should have a thorough evaluation by a doctor.

Assuming that your doctor has looked at you and determined that you have no major illnesses causing your back pain, the most likely source of your problem is one of the anatomical structures just described. Let's look at the possible causes.

Most people have heard of a "slipped disc," or a "ruptured disc." These occur when the tough, gritty structure of the disc breaks down and the jellylike center protrudes out toward the back of the body. When this happens, the disc has ruptured, or in medical terms, *herniated,* and the disc material may put pressure on a nerve to the legs.

A ruptured disc can cause back pain, but pain in the back is not the main symptom of the problem. The main indication of a ruptured disc has been described by one of my partners (who had one) as "feeling like somebody was pouring liquid nitrogen down my leg." Individuals with ruptured discs complain mainly of leg pain or discomfort—specifically, of numbness down their legs. Many people think that because they have back pain that won't go away, they must have a ruptured disc. But if you don't have leg pain, especially leg numbness, associated with this, it's very unlikely that you have a ruptured disc.

Another cause of back pain is disc degeneration. In this situation, the disc has worn out, but not severely enough that the jellylike center has ruptured outside the disc. Still, the disc has a shock absorber–like function in the back, and disc degeneration is thought to be a source of back pain. In this problem, the primary symptom is back pain. You may also have some associated leg pain, but it's unlikely you'll have a lot of numbness in the leg.

Golfers are very prone to disc problems simply because of the motion of the golf swing. A golf swing consists of a twisting motion with very high torques applied to the back. This twisting motion applies stresses to the back that are specifically absorbed by the discs. When the twisting motion applies too much stress, too much force is absorbed by the discs, and they may break down. A mild breakdown would consist only of some mild degeneration, but it eventually may develop into a complete rupture of the disc.

There are multiple other sources of back pain that affect golfers. If discs continue to degenerate over many years, arthritis may develop in those areas. This can be painful, just as arthritis is painful in other body parts. Older golfers, especially professionals, often have fairly arthritic back x-rays because the years of turning and twisting have worn out multiple areas in the back.

One arthritis-related problem that occurs in older golfers is called *spinal stenosis*. In spinal stenosis, the arthritic back develops small bone spurs that put pressure on the nerves coming from the back. The symptoms are a bit like those of a ruptured disc because this problem manifests itself mainly by pain and numbness down the legs. However, people with spinal stenosis have slightly different symptoms than people with ruptured discs, and this problem also usually rears its head in an older population. Ruptured discs are most common in people in their thirties and forties, whereas spinal stenosis usually occurs in people fifty to seventy years old.

If you ever go to a chiropractor for back pain, he or she will most likely tell you that your pain is caused by subluxations. These are subtle misalignments of the bones in the back. They are corrected by the chiropractor by manipulations, termed by many *cracking my back.*

Some medical doctors often look askance at this problem as a source of back pain because it's difficult to substantiate. However, we don't know everything about the precise sources of back pain. I wouldn't tell you that subluxations can't cause your back pain. When I played professional golf, I occasionally saw a chiropractor for back pain. Chiropractors often bring a lot of relief to people with back pain, and I'd never suggest that you shouldn't visit one. Most good chiropractors also know their limitations, and when they're not bringing a patient significant relief or when they suspect a more serious problem, such as cancer, they usually refer the patient to an orthopaedist or a neurosurgeon.

Can you get cancer in your back? Certainly. The best example recently was North Carolina State basketball coach and sportscaster Jim Valvano. Valvano went to his doctor complaining of back pain, and it turned out that he had cancer in his back. Cancer is a fairly rare source of back pain, but it's another reason you should see a doctor if you have back pain that persists and doesn't resolve itself over time. Unfortunately, most cancer in the bones of the back is not primary; that is, it's usually cancer that has spread from someplace else in the body. The most likely sources of secondary spinal cancer are the lungs, breasts, and prostate. Because the cancer has already spread from another source, secondary, or metastatic, back cancer has a very poor prognosis.

Finally, there are the soft tissues in the back—the muscles, tendons, and ligaments. Can these cause chronic back pain? It's controversial, but they probably can. If all the other sources have been eliminated, we tend to indict the soft tissues as the source of chronic back pain. That's one of the reasons we use exercise as a prescription to help overcome and prevent such pain.

The best method for avoiding back injuries or recovering from a back injury is probably a series of exercises to keep your back strong and flexible. I discussed this subject somewhat in chapter 4, but it bears repeating and expanding on.

To understand why exercise is so important, let's review the anatomy of the back. Remember the analogy in chapter 4 of the tall radio tower held in place by guy wires? The guy wires of the spine are the four sets of muscles that surround it—the muscles of your lower back (erector spinae), the muscles of your abdomen (abdominals), and the muscles along each side of your waist (the obliques). If any one of these muscle groups is much weaker than the others, the remaining muscle groups must work harder to keep the spinal tower from giving way. Also, if certain muscle groups are less flexible or tight or even if they are stretched out or too flexible, a muscle imbalance can be created. The result again is that certain muscles must work overtime to keep that tower from tumbling.

In most individuals, weakness around the waist and back lies with the abdominal muscles. In addition, if you're overweight and have a bit of a belly, the abdominals are usually stretched out and give even less support to the spine. In these cases, the muscles of the lower back and obliques must work especially hard to maintain spinal balance. This extra work places these muscles under a continual overload and may lead to their eventual failure—and to back pain.

As I said earlier, most people have relatively strong muscles in their lower back because of this abdominal weakness. The muscles are strong because they have to work so hard. But they can eventually fail. And the muscles' inherent strength may contribute, in one way, to this failure.

We talked earlier about flexibility imbalance. Most individuals have very inflexible lower back muscles, for several reasons. One is that few do stretching exercises for the lower back. Another reason is that a muscle continually working under tension (like the lower back muscles do because of abdominal weakness) becomes shorter and tighter and, therefore, less flexible. An inflexible muscle, even though it is strong, may be torn or pulled more easily, leading to muscle tears. Muscle tears heal, but with scar tissue that is inherently nonflexible, which only makes a bad situation worse.

The way to avoid this vicious circle is to keep the muscles of the lower back more flexible and the muscles of the abdomen stronger and tighter. In addition, the twisting action that golf demands with each swing is performed by and places great stress on the oblique muscles. Thus, golfers should exercise their obliques, more so than nongolfers.

Strengthening the abdominals requires some variant of the classic sit-up exercise. There are, however, some problems with the way we did sit-ups in grade school, with the legs straight and held down. Specifically, this way may not exercise the abdominals enough and may tighten some muscles around the hips, which can actually worsen back problems.

The best sit-up variant is the crunch or abdominal curl, which we described in some detail in chapter 4. The crunch specifically exercises the abdominals and doesn't place the back at risk. Build up to doing two or three sets of twenty-five crunches a day to really strengthen your abdomen.

Another excellent exercise that will both stretch the back and strengthen the abdominals is the hanging leg raise, although it's more difficult and should be done with care. If I had to choose one back exercise to do, the hanging leg raise would always be the one. Simply hang from a post, a tree limb, or a chin-up bar and pull up your knees to your chest. Hold the position as long as you can. A one-minute hold is wonderful and will provide maximum benefit. You'll feel the stretch in your lower back and the muscle tightness developing in your abdomen.

As I keep repeating, stretching out your back is extremely important. The best exercises for this are fairly simple. They consist of lying on your back and bringing your knees to your chest, either singly or both at the same time. Hurdling stretches (see Figures 4–6 and 4–7, pages 46 and 47) with straight legs are more difficult but are effective in stretching out your buttocks and lower back.

There are two excellent exercises to strengthen the obliques. The best thing about them is that they stretch one side while strengthening the other. The first exercise is the seated trunk twist (see Figure 4–3, page 44), while the second exercise for your obliques is the lateral or side bend (see Figure 4–4, page 44). When I played professional golf, I used to do these with a one-hundred-pound barbell resting on my shoulders, but it can be done with no weight, such as using a long broom handle. These are described fully in chapter 4. Again, these should be done slowly, performing from ten to twenty-five repetitions in each direction.

The aforementioned exercises are all great to strengthen your abdominals and obliques and to stretch your lower back. But be very careful. Don't do these during an attack of back pain, with the possible exception of some gentle stretching. Exercise may only aggravate the situation. When you're recovered from your back injury, you then want to go on the "back attack." Rehab those back and abdominal muscles to prevent another back injury, and get ready for better golf.

The good news is that if you have back problems or have had them, you can still play golf. Just be aware of certain swing modifications that may help you.

First, be very cautious about following the classic teachings you may read in golf magazines or even get from your golf professional. Remember that most of this instruction is aimed at players without back pain.

Specifically, the theory, promoted recently by one prominent teacher as the X-factor, espouses a large shoulder turn and a smaller hip turn. This swing style is promoted as a better way to increase distance. It probably is, and chiropractors and orthopaedists love it because it gives us a lot more business.

When you make a big shoulder turn with a small hip turn (see Figure 5–1), you're making a huge rotation in the trunk, specifically in the muscles of the back and sides. If you have poorly conditioned muscles in this

Figure 5–1
A young player
making a huge
shoulder turn,
with a smaller
hip turn—a
bad idea for
young backs.

Bill Mallon Collection/
Courtesy The Athletic
Institute and Mr.
Robert Caprera

area or if you already have back pain, you're just asking for a soft-tissue injury—or worse.

I would recommend that anyone with back problems completely disregard this advice and do exactly the opposite. I'd like to see a huge hip turn with a smaller shoulder turn. To be precise, I would encourage you to try to feel that the hips and the shoulders turn the exact same distance (see Figure 5–2). That probably won't happen because the shoulders naturally turn in a greater arc than the hips do, but that's what you

*Figure 5–2
Harry
Vardon—his
older classic
swing with a
big hip turn
will take stress
off your back.*

Bill Mallon Collection

*Figure 5–3
An older
player coming
up on his toes
at the top of the
backswing—an
ideal method to
ease pressure on
your back
muscles.*

Bill Mallon Collection

should feel. And if you feel that, you won't be setting up the resistance in the back muscles that can cause an injury or exacerbate one. It may cost you a little distance, but isn't that a small price to pay to play with less pain? And as you learn this swing, you'll time it better and likely not lose any significant distance in the long run.

To help you do this swing, you need my next bit of swing modification for golfers with bad backs. Get up on your toes! Especially the left toe on the backswing.

*Figure 5–4
A modern
player demon-
strating a
swing with a
big hip turn
and coming up
on the toes.*

Courtesy Jim Moriarty/
Mr. Ed Ibarguen

Some current teachers and players recommend keeping the left heel on the ground during the backswing, the better to increase that torque between the shoulders and hips. Letting that left heel come off the ground is the old style, we're told, used by golfers before 1900 and into the first several decades of the twentieth century. That's true. It was the method used by Harry Vardon, Walter Hagen, Bobby Jones, and Sam Snead (see Figures 5–3 and 5–4) among others. Somebody named Jack Nicklaus lets the left heel come a long way off the ground. All of them played and play pretty well, as I recall.

The "modern" style may be more efficient and may help hit the ball a bit farther by increasing the separation between the upper and lower body and producing more torque that produces a faster and more powerful unwinding of the trunk muscles. But that same torque also produces strain on the muscles, which can lead to many problems. The method is for the young limberbacks with strong, healthy back muscles. And even for them it can cause problems down the road. For most of us, the less torque the better.

So golfers with back problems should come up onto the left toe at the top of the backswing and finish by coming well up onto the right toe early into the

Figure 5–5
Finishing well
up on the right
toe will also
help your
back—don't
try to swing
flatfooted.

Courtesy Jim Moriarty/
Ms. Jaime Koizumi

follow-through. That adjustment will free up your hip turn and allow you to match your hip and shoulder turns more easily, thus greatly decreasing the stress that's placed on your lower back (see Figure 5–5).

There are a few other swing adjustments that may help you. The worst position for most people with back pain is sitting or just bending from the hips. The reasons are fairly complicated, but biomechanical analysis shows that the lower back incurs a lot of mechanical stress while sitting.

Bending from the hips creates similar problems. You're not quite sitting, but you're again placing a lot of stress on the back. To protect your back, I'd recommend bending just slightly from the hips and addressing the ball with your knees flexed more than normal. This position will place minimal stress on your back.

Now, from this position, you can't make an upright swing. The plane of your swing is determined by the angle of your back at address. With minimal bend at your hips, a flat swing is almost mandatory unless you make some other midswing adjustments, and that doesn't make for a consistent swing. A flat swing from an upright address position will put the absolute minimal stress on the muscles, ligaments, and discs in your lower back.

Many teaching pros in the 1960s and 1970s taught an extreme finish position called the "reverse-C," which I used in the halcyon days of my youth. (My spine-crunching finish is shown in Figure 5–6.) Fortunately, this position is falling out of favor. The reverse-C position results from an attempt to stay behind the ball throughout the swing. But it also places the back at great risk of injury, especially in players who play and practice a lot. The flatter swing from an erect address position

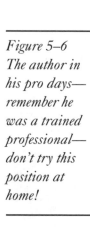

*Figure 5–6
The author in
his pro days—
remember he
was a trained
professional—
don't try this
position at
home!*

Bill Mallon Collection/
Courtesy The Athletic
Institute and Dr. Bill
Mallon

will result in a flatter, around-the-body finish with your weight balanced over your left leg and your body fairly straight up and down, putting little or no pressure on the back. You can see a nice balanced finish in Figure 5–7, which will greatly take stress off your back.

The final bit of swing advice I'll give you is to shorten your swing. Any golf swing places more stress on the back as it gets longer. Think about it—you may hurt hitting your driver, but hitting a half-wedge shot is pain free. Try to swing shorter and easier, imitating your short-iron tempo with the longer clubs. You'll not only have less pain, but also likely hit the ball farther because you're making better contact. Consequently, you'll play better.

What about neck problems, which affect many people? Let's begin by forgetting the old bromide about keeping your head down. Keep your head down, keep your head steady, don't move your head, keep your eye on the ball. Multiple variations on the same theme. Forget them all as quickly as you can.

Many great players have played, and played very well, moving their head a lot. On the current pro tours,

Figure 5–7
A nice balanced finish. This relaxed position will help you play with less back pain.

Courtesy Jim Moriarty/
Mr. Ed Ibarguen

two who come quickly to mind are Curtis Strange and Jim Colbert. Both Curtis and Jim slide to the right during their backswing, moving their head away from the ball and the target. This swing requires a bit more timing perhaps, but it places much less stress on the back. There is no dramatic twisting and turning of the back with this swing.

You may have trouble doing this adjustment—it requires some split-second timing. Even so, keeping your head dead still is not only wrong, but also dangerous and almost impossible to do. In fact, nobody keeps his or her head completely still at all times during the swing. Lets look at why this is so.

If you keep your head completely still on your shoulders during your backswing, then as your shoulders turn, your head would also turn. At the top of your backswing, your head would face completely away from the target. What occurs in every golfer's swing is that the head rotates toward the target while the shoulders rotate away from it. This movement allows you to keep "your eye on the ball."

I would prefer, however, that you keep your eye a little less on the ball and allow your head to rotate somewhat with your shoulders especially if you have neck arthritis or any neck problems at all. Trying to keep your eye on the ball is difficult with any neck problem.

The best way to accomplish this slight head rotation during your backswing is to simply do it at the beginning of your swing—at address. The best example of this movement is the greatest golfer ever, Jack Nicklaus. At address, watch Nicklaus. He cocks his head away from the target and the ball slightly. This adjustment frees his neck by "preturning" it and then allows him to make his shoulder turn with no concerns for which way his head and neck are turning.

A problem with this adjustment occurs for right-eye dominant players (among right-handed golfers). All golfers have a dominant eye. Most right-handed people are right-eye dominant. To find out your dominant eye, hold up your thumb in front of your face centered over a distant object. Close one eye and then the other. When you close your dominant eye and are viewing with your nondominant eye, the object will move away from your thumb. This precocking of the head works best for left-eyed dominant players (among right-handers).

In addition to making some changes in your swing, there are other things you can do to make it easier to play. Warming up carefully before you play is critical to any body part, perhaps more so with the back than any other area.

If you have chronic back problems, start by taking a warm shower and letting the water rain down your back. The water will warm up the muscles in your back and get them ready for the round ahead. You then need to warm up your entire body carefully by practicing on the range as I suggested earlier. Start with some simple pitches, no more than a few yards. Build up to full swings with a wedge or short iron before progressing to longer swings. And hit a few drives on the practice tee. Don't let your first full swing with a driver come on the first tee.

Before you even start hitting balls, several stretches can loosen up your back and your shoulders. Swinging two clubs very slowly will help loosen you up (see Figure 5–8). Two other stretches involve placing a club behind the back and over the shoulders and doing slow trunk twists from side to side (see Figures 5–9 and 5–10). Both exercises will help loosen up those tight back muscles.

Once on the course, get out of that cart and walk as much as possible. As I mentioned, sitting places the greatest levels of stress on a back. Walking is easier on your back, and the exercise you derive from it will bring you long-term benefits as well. You may lose some

*Figure 5–8
Warming up by
swinging two
clubs together
slowly and
gently.*

Courtesy Jim Moriarty/
Ms. Jaime Koizumi

weight. You'll strengthen your legs a bit more. And walking is just a better and more fun way to play golf.

I talked earlier about playing while standing more upright and using a flatter swing. As I discussed in chapter 3, one equipment modification you can make is to play with slightly longer clubs. These will enable you to address the ball comfortably in a more erect position.

Again, the putter, the shortest club in your bag, forces you to bend over more than any other club and

Figure 5–9 Another excellent warm-up exercise— trunk twists with a club over the shoulders.

Courtesy Jim Moriarty/
Ms. Jaime Koizumi

Figure 5–10 Trunk twists with the club behind the back will also stretch your shoulders before playing.

Courtesy Jim Moriarty/ Ms. Jaime Koizumi

puts the most strain on your back. So consider using a longer putter, either one just a few inches longer that will let you putt in a conventional manner from a more erect position or the extralong putter that is used with a pendulum style. Whichever putting style you choose, use the longest putter with which you feel comfortable.

You'll also find that bending over to take the ball out of the cup or to tee up can be difficult with back problems. What to do? To get the ball out of the cup, if you use one, have the caddy do it, as the pros do. Not many of us have that luxury, however. Bending from the knees and not from the waist is much easier on the back, so do that to get the ball out. In extreme cases, there are some attachments with a suction cup that can be put on the end of the putter to lift the ball out of the cup. Another possibility is to learn to sweep the ball out of the cup with the face of your putter, which many pros do easily. Be careful about damaging the cup, however, and don't do this unless you're able to do it easily.

Bending over to tee up the ball is a more difficult problem. I have seen some special teeing attachments, but none of them work well. Two possibilities exist. One is simply to be careful and bend from the knees and not from the waist. Another is not to tee up the ball and use a three wood or even a two wood—if you can find one.

Many players with ailing backs wear a back brace of some sort while on the golf course. This certainly does you no harm. Unfortunately, a brace doesn't lend a lot of support to the muscles of the back. But the waist-band portion of the brace will keep your back and abdominal muscles warm and probably will somewhat increase the blood supply to that area. In addition, the brace probably works by giving you what is termed *proprioceptive feedback*. Basically, it reminds you that it's there, your back is there, and your back isn't normal, so be careful.

If you're unable to play and you need to see a doctor, what will he or she do for you? First, as I described earlier, the doctor will try to make a precise diagnosis. I discussed multiple causes of back pain. The treatment of each one can be slightly different.

Your doctor will likely take a detailed history of your problem, asking many questions—whether you have leg pain, whether you smoke, what type of work you do, whether you have other medical problems, whether your back pain is associated with any problems with your bladder or bowels. All these questions are important and may lead your doctor to the correct diagnosis.

Your doctor will also perform a physical examination. Strangely, with back pain, the exam is probably less important than the history. It acts mainly as a screening tool to rule out serious medical problems and a potential loss of function.

You will likely undergo a series of x-rays or radiographs. These can locate some obvious problems, but they won't tell you whether you have a ruptured disc. X-rays can diagnose bone cancer and arthritis and certain degenerative processes in the back.

Your doctor may order some additional studies. The most commonly ordered study in the 1990s is an MRI—which stands for magnetic resonance imaging. The MRI is a special imaging test that can precisely diagnose ruptured discs, infections, and multiple other causes of back pain. MRIs are a wonderful invention, but in our crazy world of 1990s health care, they are probably overused. Everybody with back pain doesn't need an MRI. The newspaper sports pages set a bad precedent because it seems as though every injured professional athlete gets an MRI for every injury. Don't automatically assume you'll get an MRI or that you'll even need one just because you have back pain.

Once your doctor has reviewed the history of your medical problems, examined you, and ordered the appropriate studies, he or she can probably make a reasonably accurate diagnosis of the cause of your back pain. This will guide the treatment.

Most back pain from musculoskeletal causes will get better without treatment. For those with chronic back pain, this may seem an astounding statement, but it's true. More than 90 percent of back pain cases will resolve themselves in the first few weeks even if nothing is done.

More recalcitrant cases often respond to a few days of bed rest, but no more than that. The old bromide of two weeks of strict bed rest is not only without benefit, but also possibly detrimental by de-conditioning many of your muscles while you lie in bed.

You may take some medicines for your back pain. There are many different medications, but there is probably nothing much better than simple aspirin if your stomach can tolerate it. Some of the stronger anti-inflammatory medications may be prescribed and can bring some relief from pain as well. Stronger narcotic medications and muscle relaxant medications are often used to treat back pain, but they should be used only briefly and in exceptional circumstances.

It's very likely that your doctor will have you visit a physical therapist. The therapist treats back pain with a combination of modalities and exercises. Modalities involve using heat and cold, along with special machines, such as an ultrasound, electrical stimulator, or diathermy machine, which deliver the heat or cold to the deeper tissues. The exercises that the therapist will have you do are similar to the ones I described earlier. In this case, though, the therapist will guide you through the exercises, making sure you're doing them correctly and acting as a combination trainer and cheerleader.

What about chiropractic and acupuncture treatments? Earlier, we discussed chiropractors briefly. I think there's a place for chiropractic manipulation, and I think it does a lot of people a lot of good. And for lower back pain it rarely does any harm. If you have back pain that's not getting better with standard medical treatment, there's little lost from visiting a chiropractor.

Acupuncture is based on Chinese medical philosophy. In acupuncture, small needles are placed in the body along pathways, termed *meridians*, which the Chinese believe are the source of all health and all disease. By interrupting the pathways at certain points, it is felt that health can be restored. I have less experience with acupuncturists but have occasionally referred patients to them. Again, they almost certainly do no harm, and they may help.

There are other treatments for back pain, but these are reserved for more severe, long-standing cases. They include epidural steroid injections, which are cortisone shots placed around the covering of the spinal cord; facet injections, which are cortisone shots placed in some of the smaller joints of the back; and finally, surgery.

Back surgery is no panacea. Few people with back pain need back surgery. The sad truth is that not all people who undergo back surgery obtain full relief from their back pain. I'm not a big believer in second opinions if you feel your doctor is competent in his field, but I'd always get a second opinion before considering any back surgery. I'd also ask the surgeon to be honest—what are the possible results? What has been his experience in the past? What are the chances that you will improve? Will you get back to golf? These are difficult questions, and the answers may be harder. There are few guarantees with back surgery. There have been several well-known professionals who have undergone back surgery and recovered to again play the game well—Lee Trevino, George Archer, Fuzzy Zoeller, and Dan Pohl come quickly to mind. But there have been many other golfers at all levels for whom surgery was not the answer.

So if your back hurts, you have a lot of company. That may not give you much solace, but you may be reassured by knowing you probably can continue to play golf. As I've indicated, there are things you can do to relieve your back pain and ways to play golf to prevent the problem from recurring. Don't give up—there's hope!

6

Shoulders

Shoulder injuries in golfers are common. In frequency, they trail back and elbow injuries among golfers in most studies, and they occur about as often as hand and wrist problems. There are a number of factors that cause shoulder injuries, starting with the necessity for professionals and competitive amateurs to practice many hours a day, which can lead to a cumulative trauma disorder.

Even if you don't fall into one of those groups, and most of you probably don't, the biomechanics of the golf swing put the shoulder, particularly the left shoulder (in right-handed players), at risk of injury. If you think about it, the left arm of a right-handed golfer crosses completely across the chest while it's being raised. It's an unusual action that, when done at higher speeds and done repetitively, puts the shoulder in jeopardy. That's why the lead shoulder is injured far more often than the trail shoulder.

Golfers sustain injuries to the shoulder that are unique to the sport. I'll discuss these injuries and what you can do to overcome and prevent them.

Rotator Cuff Injuries

If you are even a casual reader of the newspaper sports pages, you've heard of the rotator cuff. Most likely, however, you have no idea what it is except that it's something in the shoulder. But baseball players, quarterbacks, and even golfers injure the rotator cuff often. And the injury is by no means limited to athletes. It also commonly occurs in older people. Like wear-and-tear arthritis, it's a disease of old age in which the rotator cuff literally wears out. So if you're a golfer with a few years on you, you're a candidate.

The rotator cuff is a series of four muscles that surrounds the bone of the upper arm (the humerus) like a cuff and helps to rotate the arm at the shoulder. Several things can occur to cause rotator cuff problems.

The most common problem is tendinitis. In this situation, the rotator cuff becomes inflamed and painful. Raising the arm is especially painful, although often, a person will have pain only through a short arc of elevation, sometimes termed *painful arc syndrome*. Also, many times the pain is worse when lying down, especially at night, because lying down causes blood to drain toward the shoulder, causing it to swell and hurt even worse.

Many people, when they incur such pain, believe they have bursitis in their shoulders, and this can be true. A bursa is a fluid-filled sac that, in this case, overlies the tendons of the rotator cuff. It also can become inflamed and filled with fluid, which causes pain. The tendons and the bursa are so close together that many times, the two problems coexist.

A more difficult problem occurs when the rotator cuff tears apart completely. Although the sportswriters talk about this happening to athletes often, this scenario isn't common. A rotator cuff tear, again, happens more often in older individuals. It's usually a degenerative process in which the rotator cuff eventually tears from years of attrition. Usually, but not always, a torn rotator cuff is preceded by warning signs of painful tendinitis or bursitis.

So how do you tell whether you have rotator cuff problems? One clue can be your age. A rotator cuff injury is by far the most common cause of shoulder pain in somebody more than thirty and especially more than forty years old. In younger age groups, the problem is more often that of an unstable shoulder. If you have pain in your shoulder with muscular activity, if it hurts to raise the arm above shoulder level, if you have a painful arc of elevation, if your shoulder hurts worse at night, and, especially, if you're more than forty years old, you should suspect a rotator cuff problem.

Could it be anything else? Yes, it could, and in any event, you should have a chronically painful shoulder evaluated by a doctor. One very important point to remember is that heart problems can cause shoulder pain, most commonly in the left shoulder, although it can occur in either. The key to watch for here is muscular activity of the shoulder versus aerobic activity. If your left shoulder pain occurs only while walking, especially upstairs or uphill or while doing other vigorous activity not involving your arms, and the pain doesn't occur when you're using your arms for athletic endeavors, then you should get to a cardiologist and be checked out quickly.

Now that you've established that the problem is your rotator cuff, what do you do? First, don't think immediately that you need surgery. You most likely don't. Most rotator cuff problems are simply overuse injuries that respond to the standard sports medicine protocols of rest, ice, compression, and elevation (RICE). Avoiding painful activities for a few weeks to rest your shoulder is often all the treatment you need. Applying ice when it hurts also will help decrease inflammation. Compression and elevation are difficult in the shoulder, but elevation can be achieved if necessary by sleeping sitting up or in a recliner or on several pillows propped up.

The next most common treatment for rotator cuff problems involves exercise and often an anti-inflammatory medication. Most orthopaedists will start their patients with rotator cuff injuries on a rehab protocol aimed at strengthening certain muscles around their shoulder and also stretching certain muscles. Many rotator cuff problems respond nicely to this treatment.

Anti-inflammatory medication can be as simple as aspirin or other over-the-counter medications now available, such as Advil, Nuprin, Motrin, or Aleve. In more severe cases, many prescription anti-inflammatory medicines can be tried. One caution: All these medications cause possible stomach upset and even an ulcer if used excessively. If you have an ulcer or have had one, don't use these medicines without being under a doctor's care. A history of kidney problems is another reason to avoid their use unless prescribed by your doctor and used with care.

If your rotator cuff is causing you shoulder pain, do you have to stop playing golf? No, but you may need to take a short break to rest your shoulder and allow it time to recover.

*Figure 6–1
A young
player with an
upright arm
swing, which
may place
excess stress
on painful
rotator cuffs.*

Courtesy Jim Moriarty/
Ms. Jaime Koizumi

If you choose to play, there are certain swing modifications you can make to avoid pressure on the rotator
cuff. Remember that elevation of the arm usually causes
the rotator cuff to hurt (see Figure 6–1). That position
should be avoided. The best way to do this is to shorten
your backswing and keep it slightly flatter (see Figure
6–2). Both a long backswing and an upright one will
cause your hands to become more elevated, potentially
hurting your rotator cuff. As I said earlier, most golfers

*Figure 6–2
Keeping the
swing plane
flatter will help
take stress off
the rotator cuff.*

Courtesy Jim Moriarty/
Mr. Ed Ibarguen

with rotator cuff problems get them in the lead arm, or left arm for right-handed players. The trail arm is relatively protected, so few adjustments are usually needed in the downswing or follow-through.

If you want to keep playing with rotator cuff problems, try those swing adjustments. But even more important, be certain to warm up your shoulder carefully before playing. Do some gentle stretching exercises to loosen your shoulders. Make sure you hit a few balls on the practice tee before going out to play, starting with short clubs and easy swings. Things like deep-heating salves and creams also may help keep your shoulders warm while playing. After playing, put some ice on your shoulder quickly to lessen any inflammation.

Many orthopaedists treat rotator cuff problems with physical therapy, and you may benefit from this as well. Physical therapy of the shoulder is quite complicated. The therapy consists of strengthening certain muscles about your shoulder while stretching other muscles. This approach takes stress off the rotator cuff and may allow you to play without further treatment. Later in this chapter, we outline an exercise program for your shoulders that may help you.

What if all the above fails to improve your shoulder problems? Can you try a cortisone shot? Yes, you can, and it's often used by many doctors. Remember, cortisone doesn't actually heal anything in your shoulder, however; and it may only mask the symptoms long enough for the shoulder to heal on its own. It can be dramatically successful at doing that. A word of caution: One or two cortisone shots spread out over several months is okay, but be extremely careful of having more than that. Overuse of cortisone actually can do more harm than good.

If everything else fails, you may consider surgery on your shoulder. Before doing this, your orthopaedic surgeon will likely order some special x-ray studies of your shoulder to determine whether you actually have a torn rotator cuff. In the 1970s this was almost always a study called an arthrogram, in which dye was injected into the shoulder and then special x-rays were made. Today, it's more often an MRI or an ultrasound study of the shoulder. Either is very effective.

Is there any way to tell whether your shoulder simply has tendinitis or whether the rotator cuff is actually torn? There are some ways to tell, but patients usually can't. Doctors will look for some subtle changes on x-rays as well as looking for weakness in certain movements around the shoulder. Still, in many cases, orthopaedists prefer to get that MRI or ultrasound to make certain.

If you elect to have surgery on your shoulder, you certainly will have many questions. My subspecialty is shoulder surgery, and by now I expect these questions. After years of practice, I have fairly good answers to them. Remember, however, that each patient is different, and the answers may vary according to your specific problem, your lifestyle, your general health, and even your job.

If your rotator cuff is not torn but your shoulder is simply not improving, your orthopaedist may recommend an *acromioplasty*. In this operation, a portion of the bone overlying the rotator cuff is removed to take pressure off the cuff and help decrease any mechanical impingement that may be causing the tendinitis. The operation historically has been done by an open procedure, with about a one-and-a-half-inch incision, but it now can be done arthroscopically. There is probably no major difference in the effectiveness of either method, although you may recover slightly faster from arthroscopic surgery. After this operation, it usually takes from six to twelve weeks to return to the golf course.

If you have a complete rotator cuff tear and you elect to have it repaired, your recovery will be slower. The operation is virtually always done with an open incision and involves pulling the tendon back down into the bone and holding it there with sutures. Thus, recovery and rehab is slower because the tendon and sutures have to remain attached to the bone. You shouldn't expect to play golf any earlier than three months or, more likely, six months after this operation. It may take a full year to completely recover from a rotator cuff repair.

Both the acromioplasty and the rotator cuff repair can be done on an outpatient basis, although many times patients will be admitted to the hospital overnight for the acromioplasty and two days for the repair surgery because it is more extensive. How long you'll be out of work depends on your job and whether the surgery was on your dominant arm. Individuals who work at a desk may be able to return in three or four days, using a sling, but if the surgery is on the dominant arm, it may take a little longer. Individuals with more demanding jobs can expect to be out at least several weeks.

The results of both surgeries are usually quite good. Most patients obtain relief from pain and recover full motion of the shoulder. More questionable is the return of strength in cases of rotator cuff tears. Except in instances of very large rotator cuff tears, most golfers eventually will be able to return to the course. Recovery depends on you. It will take time, rehabilitation, and practice, but it can be done.

Acromio-Clavicular Joint Injuries

Although the rotator cuff is the most frequent source of shoulder pain in golfers, it's not the only one. Golfers also develop pain in their acromio-clavicular joint, known to surgeons as the AC joint. This joint is at the top of the shoulder where the end of the collarbone meets the top of the shoulder blade.

It's been known for several years that this joint is frequently injured by football players, hockey players, and cyclists (from falls), and more recently, it has been shown to develop degenerative arthritis in weightlifters. Within the last year, however, we have discovered that this joint may also cause problems in golfers.

I can tell you that this is a common source of shoulder pain in golfers who play or practice often. Again, it usually occurs in the left shoulder because of the high stress placed on the joint at the top of the backswing that I discussed earlier. My conjecture is that, as with weightlifters, it's a degenerative process that occurs in better players who have had to hit thousands of balls to become and remain better players. In some of my golfing patients, they have already developed frank arthritis of this joint that required treatment.

Unfortunately, once you have this problem, it's often progressive. Treatment can be with aspirin-like medications or ice packs after playing. Occasionally, a cortisone shot is injected into the joint to provide temporary relief. The surgical treatment involves removing about the last one and a half inches of the end of the collarbone or clavicle. This removes the arthritic portion of the bone and is usually highly successful.

Yes, the surgery can be done arthroscopically, although not a lot of orthopaedic surgeons do it this way yet. Even as an open procedure, the surgery takes less than thirty minutes, and the incision is no more than an inch.

Golf is certainly possible after the surgery, and you should even be able to play better because your pain has been relieved. To date, I have performed the surgery on six professional or competitive, low-handicap golfers (and many others), all with good results. The function of the shoulder after such surgery is usually fairly normal, and there's no reason it would harm a player's golf game.

I cannot think of major changes in your golf swing that will significantly help this problem. Shortening the backswing may help a little. Another swing move that may cause pain in the AC joint is keeping your left arm very close to your chest during your backswing. Although not usually recommended by professionals, if you have pain in your AC joint, you may benefit by keeping some space between your left arm and your chest during your backswing.

Shoulder Instability

The most common cause of shoulder pain in young people (under thirty) is shoulder instability. All of us have heard of people whose shoulders go out of joint frequently. This disabling problem often requires surgery. But in addition to these people with gross shoulder instability, there are many other young people whose shoulder joints are simply "loose."

Many of the better young players I see and treat have this problem. Shoulders may become unstable in several different directions. The most common instability is what we term *anterior*, or toward the front of the body. This is the standard direction in which most shoulders dislocate. However, the shoulder may dislocate posteriorly, or toward the back. A very difficult problem, called multidirectional instability, is one in which the shoulder is unstable in several different directions.

I've never heard of anybody fully dislocating a shoulder from a golf swing. The players I see with this problem typically are fairly young—often college golfers—and relate some episode of popping, clicking, or clunking during the golf swing. With this noisy shoulder comes a sudden, sharp pain, along with subsequent difficulty in swinging and playing. The problem is a subtle one, because it's critically important to determine whether the shoulder is actually unstable, and if it is, in which direction the instability is occurring.

I diagnose this in my office in a far different manner than most orthopaedists. I stand behind the golfer and have the person imitate his or her golf swing while I place my hand on the left shoulder. (The problem has invariably occurred in the left shoulder of right-handed players.) At a certain point in the swing, I can often feel and hear the click or clunk or at least the player can then tell me when it's happening, and I can get some feel for what is going on in the shoulder.

Pain early in the forward swing is an unusual occurrence. Usually these patients have posterior instability of the shoulder that became evident with a palpable clunk during the beginning of the forward swing. What is occurring is complicated in the telling, but it seems that during the backswing the left shoulder goes into a position in which it slips slightly out of the back of the joint. At the beginning of the forward swing, the shoulder suddenly pops back into the joint, causing the loud click or clunk and the pain in the shoulder.

Pain in the left shoulder near the end of the follow-through may occur from symptoms of anterior instability. This common position, with the left arm up in the air and almost behind the player's shoulder, is one in which shoulders often dislocate or go partially out of joint.

Quite frankly, when I walk into an examining room to see a new patient with a shoulder problem, I love it when they tell me, "Doc, my shoulder comes out of joint." Most of my problems are over because the patient has made the diagnosis for me.

Unstable shoulders are difficult problems. We usually try to treat them with exercise and rehabilitation. This approach works fairly well for shoulders that are posteriorly unstable (go out the back) or for multidirectional instability. But shoulders with anterior instability don't respond well to rehab and often need surgery. Medicines likely will not help at all except occasionally to ease some of the pain caused by the instability.

There is no place for a cortisone injection in an unstable shoulder. If your doctor is recommending a cortisone shot as a treatment, you probably should get a second opinion. The reason is that the problem is mechanical, the ball and socket joint of the shoulder is not working right. The socket is no longer containing the ball. Cortisone works by decreasing inflammation. Instability is not a problem of inflammation; thus the cortisone cannot solve the problem in any way.

How do you deal with your golf swing and make adjustments to play with an unstable shoulder? Probably the only thing that will work is to shorten your swing significantly. If you feel pain and a pop or clunk at the top of your backswing, you should suspect posterior instability and should shorten your backswing. If the pain and symptoms of instability occur at the finish of your swing, try to learn to swing like Tom Wargo, the Senior Tour star, with a markedly abbreviated follow-through.

Preventing Shoulder Injuries with Exercise and Swing Modifications

One of the causes of injury in sports is often poor technique. As I mentioned in chapter 4, several medical studies have shown that professional golfers use a much lower percentage of their muscular potential during the swing than amateurs do but still generate more club head speed. Their technique is better, which allows them to use the muscles in their bodies more efficiently.

Any golfer with a chronic injury may want to seek out his golf professional and discuss the problem. Your pro may be able to teach you ways to swing that will take stress off the painful body part, particularly the shoulder. Simply learning a better, more efficient swing may take stress off the injured shoulder—and everything else.

The next trick to avoid shoulder injuries, or playing well in spite of them, is to warm up carefully, which is really only the common-sense approach I've discussed before. Warming up for at least thirty minutes before playing a round of golf is done by all professional golfers and should be done by anyone who is going to put his body to the stress of a round of golf.

If you can't hit balls at your golf facility, at least try the three warm-up exercises demonstrated in Figures 5–8 through 5–10 (pages 83–85). In Figure 5–8, you loosen up like baseball players, simply by swinging two or three clubs held together. Swing these very slowly and easily. Use them only to warm up, not to build strength or prove you're macho. If you don't swing multiple clubs easily, you may risk injury rather than help prevent it.

In the second exercise (see Figure 5–9), the club is held behind the shoulders, and the trunk is rotated from side to side, imitating a shoulder turn. This movement primarily warms up the back. In Figure 5–10, the club is placed behind the back, and the hands grip the club with the arms fully extended. The trunk is then rotated in both directions, which loosens up the back and the shoulders. This last exercise is especially good for stretching and warming up your shoulders.

Flexibility and strength in the shoulders are very important and can be developed in several ways. Perhaps the ultimate exercise for developing shoulder and back flexibility for golfers is to swing a weighted club, as we discussed in chapter 4.

Strengthening the shoulders to prevent injury definitely involves building up the muscles of the rotator cuff. These muscles don't respond well to traditional weight training—military presses, bench presses, or deltoid raises. If you really need significant rotator-cuff strengthening, you will likely benefit from visiting a physical therapist and getting a specific program to strengthen these muscles.

The normally weak external rotators are stressed in most programs. An easy exercise that can be done at home is to lie on your side, with the arm you wish to exercise away from the floor or bench. Use a dumbbell or a small weight (5 to 10 lbs. is plenty) in your hand. Keep your elbow against the side of your body, your forearm lying across your waist with your elbow bent 90°. Then slowly rotate the weight away from your waist and up away from the floor, all the time keeping your elbow at your side. An excellent workout will consist of three sets of ten repetitions of this exercise.

Most shoulder rehabilitation programs use various forms of push-ups with the hands very close together. An excellent exercise for golfers with shoulder problems is *wall push-ups,* in which you put your hands together on a wall and your feet about two feet away from the wall. Lower yourself toward the wall and then push yourself away.

Rowing exercises, done on a machine you can buy for your home (unless you live on a lake and own a rowboat) are also excellent. They strengthen the muscles around the shoulder blade (scapula) and help stabilize the shoulder, providing a less painful, better-functioning shoulder and more normal shoulder rhythm.

Finally, stretching your shoulder should finish any shoulder workout. The best way to stretch is with a towel, a wooden dowel, or even a golf club. Place the towel, dowel, or club behind your back. Grab one end with one hand down below your waist and the other end with your opposite hand up over your shoulder. Then use each hand to pull against the other, both strengthening and stretching the shoulders.

The shoulder is a commonly injured area for golfers. To avoid injuring this area, warm up carefully, keep the muscles around your shoulders strong, and keep your backswing slightly shorter and slightly flatter. You'll play longer and with less pain.

7

Golfers' Elbows

After the back, the most commonly injured area for golfers is the elbow. There are several reasons for this injury, although only a few different problems commonly occur in golfers' elbows.

By far, the most common elbow problem in golfers is tendinitis. Actually, it's more correct to say that golfers get a lot of tennis elbow! Tennis elbow is technically called lateral epicondylitis.

Feel your elbow and you'll find a little bone, called the lateral epicondyle, on the outside portion. About half the forearm muscles are attached to that bone by a fairly small tendon. When those tendons get inflamed and become painful and tender, lateral epicondylitis has reared its ugly head, although it's really just a variation of tendinitis.

Is there such a thing as golfer's elbow? Yes, there is. But even though that term has been applied to a certain elbow injury, it's really a misnomer. Golfers get tennis elbow far more than they get golfer's elbow—the ratio is about four to one in my experience and according to some other published studies.

Golfers' elbow is technically medial epicondylitis, but it is again a variation of tendinitis. Feel the little bone on the inside of your elbow, nearest your rib cage just above your funny bone (which is actually a large nerve). This little bone is the medial epicondyle, and the other half of the forearm muscles are attached to this bone by another small tendon.

Lateral and medial epicondylitis are the most common elbow injuries sustained by golfers. There are some other rare causes of elbow pain, but they're not specifically related to golf injuries. These include arthritis, loose bodies, and damage to that nerve (the ulnar nerve) near your medial epicondyle.

Golfers get tendinitis about the elbow for the same reason tennis players do. The forearm muscles are fairly large, and they are connected to those bones by some fairly small tendons. At impact, and even during the swing if you have a firm grip, a lot of force is transmitted to the forearm muscles. This force is then transmitted to the tendons about the elbow, but because the tendons are much smaller than the muscles, this force is multiplied many times, and a significant shock is registered on the tendons exactly where they attach to the bones at the elbow. When this shock is repeated many times or the golfer has poor mechanics or weak forearm muscles, it's an invitation to develop elbow tendinitis.

Golfers almost always develop elbow problems in the lead elbow or the left elbow for right-handed golfers, because it is kept straighter throughout the swing and absorbs more of the shock of impact than the trailing elbow does.

Because a primary cause of tendinitis is that the force of the grip and impact is transmitted through your forearm muscles to those small tendons, the best way to prevent or avoid elbow problems is to build up those muscles. The larger and stronger the forearm muscles are, the more they will absorb the shock of impact and the pressure of your grip, without transmitting excessive shock to your elbow.

You need a forearm that looks like Rod Laver's, the former tennis great. Laver so developed his tennis forearm that he was once described by a sportswriter as "the body dangling by a forearm." But in his long career, he never developed elbow pain. Laver used a technique that everyone can do—he simply squeezed a tennis ball continuously to strengthen his forearm. Even busy executives or professionals can do this exercise during the week to prevent elbow problems from occurring on the weekends. Keep a tennis ball or a rubber ball by your desk, and use your left hand to squeeze it for five or ten minutes at a time while you're talking on the phone or anytime you're not using both your hands. It's a good way to relieve some stress, too!

Other forearm exercises can be done with barbells or dumbbells and will strengthen your wrist and forearms. These are demonstrated in chapter 4 and in Figures 4–9 through 4–13. They are called wrist curls and reverse wrist curls. In wrist curls (see Figure 4–9, page 48), a barbell is lowered to the end of the fingertips, then the fingers curl the weight back into the palm. In the reverse wrist curl (see Figures 4–10 and 4–11, page 50), the palms face down while holding the barbell, and the exercise involves lifting the hands upward while keeping your forearms resting on your thighs. A final exercise is termed a wrist roller. The wrist roller (see Figures 4–12 and 4–13, page 50) is performed using a bar connected to a weight by a rope. By rolling up the weight until the rope is fully wound around the bar, you'll really give your forearms a workout.

All golfers who tend to have elbow pain should become familiar with these exercises. The weight you use has to be determined individually. I'd recommend starting each exercise by doing one set of about ten repetitions, using a weight you can handle comfortably. Eventually, build up to doing three sets of ten to fifteen reps for each exercise. Of the three, the wrist roller may be the most difficult to do with elbow problems. You'll need to be careful with this one.

Most weight exercises should only be done every other day to allow the muscles to recover. However, forearms are tough because we use them so much every day. They can stand everyday workouts if they are not already injured. *Don't* do these exercises when your elbow is hurting a lot. The muscles then need some rest and time to recover. *You don't want to exercise an already inflamed tendon and add to the problem.*

––––––––––

If you develop elbow tendinitis or other elbow injuries, there are things you can do with your golf swing for protection. Again, you'll need to forget some of the classic teachings about golf swings. While they may be great for learning to play like a professional, they're also a little harder on your body. If you're not a twenty-year-old limberback trying to get on the pro tour, a few swing modifications can definitely help you play with less pain.

First, I'd absolutely forget about playing with a straight left arm. That practice gets orthopaedic surgeons a lot of business! Keeping the left arm fully straight on the backswing and into impact is an invitation to disaster—or at least surgery.

Many professionals play with a bent left elbow. The best ones that come to mind are Curtis Strange and Johnny Miller. Jim Colbert, the Senior Tour star, bends his left arm noticeably at the top of the backswing. Steve Melnyk, now a TV golf commentator, who won the 1969 U.S. Amateur and played for more than a decade on the PGA Tour, bent his left arm drastically on the backswing and played very well with it. Coincidentally, Melnyk later developed elbow problems that shortened his career, but only after falling on his arm and breaking his elbow.

In addition, two famous players could not fully straighten their left arms. One was Ed Furgol, whose left arm was withered and bent, but he played well enough to win the 1954 U.S. Open. The other, Calvin Peete, broke his left arm as a child and is unable to fully straighten it. Nevertheless, he was one of the best players in the world in the 1980s and is now playing successfully on the Senior Tour.

In fact, very few if any Tour professionals and top amateurs keep their left arms rigidly straight on the backswing, which should put an end to that old teaching gospel. I don't mean to imply that your left arm should bend to ninety degrees, although some old-timers like Harry Vardon and Walter Hagen played pretty well that way. The key words here are tension and relaxation. I would like your left arm to have as little tension as possible during your backswing and near impact. To accomplish this, it must be fairly relaxed. If you can keep your left arm straight with minimal tension on the muscles, so much the better. Few people can. Nor do you have to. A left arm that is bent at the top of the backswing will straighten naturally into the impact zone because of the centrifugal force created by the swinging club head (see Figure 7–1).

Tension in the arm leads to tightness of the forearm and wrist muscles. This tightness will lead to increased

Figure 7–1 A comfortably bent elbow— the best way to take stress off painful elbows.

Courtesy Jim Moriarty/ Mr. Ed Ibarguen

*Figure 7–2
A young pro
demonstrating
a rigid left
elbow—
a good way to
develop elbow
tendinitis.*

Bill Mallon Collection/
Courtesy The Athletic
Institute and Dr. Bill
Mallon

strain at the top of the backswing and the change of direction into the forward swing. You then have increased shock at impact and the likelihood that the forces of the golf swing will be transmitted more directly and forcibly to the tendons at the elbow. If you play a lot of golf, this chain reaction sets up a major risk in developing tennis elbow, or tendinitis at the elbow (see Figure 7–2).

Second, if you have elbow problems, strengthen your grip unless you already have a very strong grip. By a strong grip I mean one in which the left hand is turned more to the right (for a right-hander) when it's placed on the club. A weak grip, one in which the left hand is turned more to the left on the club, requires you to rotate your forearms very quickly through impact to avoid hitting the ball to the right. By strengthening your grip, you'll be able to hit the ball straight with less forearm rotation, again taking stress off your elbows.

One caution—if you already hit the ball fairly straight with a weaker grip, be certain to allow for a bit of a hook when you first strengthen your grip. You also may lose a little distance at first because of that decrease in your forearm rotation, which slows down your release a bit at impact. This situation translates initially into less club head speed, but you will get back the speed as your swing adjusts to a stronger grip.

The other grip modification you need to make is to play with a very "light" grip. I don't mean "loose." You should hold the club as firmly as possible without creating tension. Sam Snead once described the amount of force you should use in gripping a club as "enough to hold on to a little bird." That way, the grip is firm enough to keep the bird from flying away but not so firm that you'll hurt it. Keep that thought in mind to keep your grip light and decrease tension in your forearm muscles.

It's not enough simply to have a light grip pressure at address. You should try to keep that light grip pressure constant throughout the swing. Your grip pressure will tighten instinctively as you begin the swing because the weight of the club forces it to (and that little bird in your hands will become a dead bird, incidentally, at the finish of a full swing). But you should feel that the grip remains as light as possible and doesn't change pressure at any stage of the swing.

Spend time on the range practicing hitting balls with a light grip throughout your swing. It takes some work at first. But a light grip will not only decrease stress in your forearm muscles and stave off elbow pain, but also make your swing more consistent and effective by decreasing tension in your arms, allowing them to swing more freely.

Elbow problems can especially be painful at the moment of impact especially if you're taking big divots. All golfers with elbow problems need to learn a more sweeping action to hit the ball with less pain. Try this experiment if you have elbow pain—hit two balls, one off a tee with a sweeping action and one off the ground with a more descending swing that takes a big divot. You'll notice a difference immediately. Sweeping the ball away can make anyone with elbow pain play more comfortably. You can do this action in several ways: by making sure there's not too much weight on your left foot at address, by positioning the ball a little more forward in your stance at address, or by flattening your swing plane a bit. If you're having problems, consult your golf professional, and tell him or her what you're trying to do.

If your elbow already hurts and you still want to play, what can you do about it? You may want to visit your doctor for some advice. That likely will help, and I'll discuss shortly what a doctor might do for you. Absent that, you probably can continue playing with some modifications if you're not hurting too much and if you don't mind a little pain. It's unlikely that you'll

Figure 7–3
A ball lying on
a rock. Unless
you're playing
golf profession-
ally, this is a
good time to . . .

Courtesy Jim Moriarty

do any long-term damage if you use a little common sense before and during your round.

First, warm up carefully before playing, concentrating on the elbow. I'd run some hot water over the elbow before going out to play. Heat is beneficial when you're hurting. These days, everybody recommends ice, ice, ice, but that should come mostly after playing or exercising, when you're hurting more and the elbow may be more inflamed. Before playing, you want the elbow

Figure 7–4
. . . take a drop,
as this golfer is
demonstrating.

Courtesy Jim Moriarty/
Ms. Jaime Koizumi

warm to increase blood flow to the area, and heat will work better. Also, keep the elbow warm while you're playing. An elbow sleeve, either neoprene or elastic, may keep some warmth in the forearm, elbow muscles, and tendons, and may help a bit.

After those initial warm-up preparations, don't run out to the first tee and whack your drive as hard as you can. First, warm up a bit on the practice tee, hitting short shots, little pitches, and working up to longer shots, as I've discussed earlier. Sweep the ball as much as possible on the practice tee. Even use a tee for your iron shots if you want. Don't aggravate the situation before you get started.

During your round, remember the discussion on sweeping the ball and other swing modifications—bend your left arm, use a strong grip, and keep your grip pressure light. The best way to sweep the ball is simply to tee it up on every shot—if your opponents are kindhearted and will agree to it in a friendly match. And good luck with that! I'm sure you'll have to give away a few extra strokes in return.

Second, when you're playing, don't be a hero. If your ball is lying next to a root or a rock (see Figure 7–3), move it and take a drop (see Figure 7–4). Even if you have to take a penalty stroke, move it! Hitting those shots is heroic and looks great on television. But if you're a fourteen handicapper with a painful elbow and are simply trying to enjoy a round of golf, it's simply stupid.

Finally, if you have chronic elbow problems, you may get some help by making adjustments in your equipment, as I discussed in chapter 3. I say this, however, with reservation. You may benefit from playing with graphite shafts as opposed to steel. The graphite shaft manufacturers promote these shafts as instrumental in lessening shock, and that may be true. I emphasize that it may be true because no scientific studies have shown that graphite shafts transmit less shock to your elbows.

Still, it is certain that graphite is no worse than steel, and it may provide some protection against elbow problems. A few of the professionals on tour who have had elbow injuries swear by them. Empirically, then, I'd say that graphite shafts probably help a little. If they are in your price range, you may want to try them.

What will your doctor do for your elbow problem? First, I'll assume that your problem is lateral epicondylitis or tennis elbow. As I said, this is, by far, the most common elbow malady golfers suffer. This being the case, your doctor may tell you to quit playing golf awhile, and that may be good advice. If you have recently injured your elbow and the pain has just started, you'll likely benefit from a short rest. This will help decrease the inflammation in the injured area.

You're also likely to be advised to try an anti-inflammatory medication, either by prescription or in an over-the-counter drug such as Advil, Ibuprofen, Aleve, and Nuprin. Actually, if your stomach can tolerate it, aspirin may be as good as anything else in relieving inflammation.

Doctors also make ample use of modalities—specifically, procedures involving ice and heat. If you are referred to a physical therapist, the therapist may also use more advanced modalities such as ultrasound, electrical stimulation, and diathermy, all of which help heat the muscles and soft tissues deeper than simple heat. These devices deliver increased blood supply to the inflamed area and may promote healing.

As I mentioned earlier, before playing or using your arms actively, heat is the preferred treatment because it warms the injured area and promotes blood flow. But after exercise or immediately after an injury, ice is more effective. It decreases inflammation and swelling and allows the injured area to heal more rapidly.

An effective treatment for tennis elbow is a tennis elbow brace. Your doctor will likely suggest you use one, and if he doesn't, ask about one. A tennis elbow brace consists of a simple strap wrapped around the forearm just below the elbow and held in place with Velcro. The brace works by absorbing the shock in the forearm muscles before it gets to the elbow and the injured tendons. And you can play golf easily while wearing one. All golfers with elbow tendinitis probably should use a brace while playing.

If your problem is more persistent, there are two other options: a cortisone injection to the elbow and surgery. The use of cortisone injections is controversial, and some doctors won't use them. There is minimal short-term risk in a cortisone shot, but repeated cortisone injections should be avoided. They can lead to some tendon degeneration and may even cause a tendon to rupture or tear.

I give cortisone injections for elbow tendinitis, but I limit the number I give to no more than two in the same region except in rare circumstances. If you need more cortisone injections than that, you should consider a different treatment. It is also not certain how cortisone works. It decreases inflammation and may allow the tendon to heal simply by relieving your pain while the healing process occurs. In some people, however, the cortisone gives only transient relief.

Surgery for tennis elbow, or lateral epicondylitis, should be reserved for last if all other treatments have failed. Various surgical options are available, but the most common procedure involves a release of the tendon from the bone at the elbow. There's usually some injured tissue there that's removed, and the tendon is then reattached to the bone. This procedure is usually done as outpatient surgery with a local or regional anesthesia. You don't need to be put to sleep.

Unfortunately, the rehabilitation period for tennis elbow surgery is usually three to six months. So if you need it, plan it carefully, and expect to be off the course awhile.

Cubital Tunnel Syndrome

If you have pain in the elbow that causes numbness going down the forearm to the little and ring fingers, you may be a victim of cubital tunnel syndrome. This pain is caused by an inflammation of the nerve behind the inside of your elbow, technically called the ulnar nerve but usually known as the funny bone. It's the elbow nerve one hits that causes the hand to "go to sleep." This nerve supplies sensation to the little finger and to part of the ring finger. When inflamed, those fingers often become numb. The nerve also supplies many of the small muscles of the hand that control a golf grip. When the nerve is severely damaged, those muscles may become weakened, making control of the club difficult.

Cubital tunnel syndrome is similar to the better-known carpal tunnel syndrome, which is compression of a nerve at the wrist. In this case, it involves compression of the ulnar nerve at the elbow. Treatment usually begins with resting the inflamed area. Elbow pads may be used for people who are damaging the nerve by leaning or lying on it. Often, these pads need to be used at night to avoid placing pressure on the nerve while sleeping.

If rest does not provide relief, elbow splints may be used to immobilize the area to allow even more rest to the inflamed nerve. These are usually supplemented by certain medications similar to aspirin or Advil. Tennis elbow braces may occasionally help but are usually used for true tennis elbow. Unfortunately, this brace may occasionally exacerbate the problem. If all else fails, certain surgical procedures can be performed to release pressure on the nerve.

It should also be remembered that there are other causes of elbow pain and hand numbness. Specifically, neck problems may mimic the syndrome you have described, and the neck should be carefully examined.

So like the other ailments I discuss in the book, elbow problems are common and can be dealt with. If you get the proper treatment and use common sense, you can relieve your pain and keep playing.

8

Hand and Wrist Problems

Anthropologists tell us that only two things truly separate humans from their ancestors, the apes: the brain and the hand. The human hand is an amazingly versatile, complex structure. With it, our species has created great works of art and music, performed delicate surgery and amazing athletic feats. But because of its complexity and ensuing delicacy, the hand also occasionally sustains severe injuries.

You might suppose that golfers incur more hand and wrist injuries than all other body parts combined. After all, the hand grips the club and absorbs all the shock of impact. Strangely, hand and wrist problems rank behind the back and elbow and about even with the shoulder in frequency of problems among golfers.

Golfers, of course, suffer from many of the same hand and wrist problems sustained by the general population. They also incur some injuries common to the sport.

Which Grip Is Best

Let's discuss grip positions that can reduce the chances of injury while swinging the golf club or that can help overcome the injuries once they have occurred.

The standard grip has many variations. A weak grip means the left hand is turned more to the left. A strong grip means it's turned more to the right. You can use a "long thumb," which means your left thumb (for right-handers) is extended down the handle of the club. Or you can use a "short thumb," which means the left thumb is held snugly on the club handle. You also can use an interlocking, overlapping, and ten-finger grip or any variation of these.

All these variations probably don't make much difference in preventing or overcoming hand and wrist injuries. The grip is, largely, a matter of personal preference.

What's important is how firmly you hold the club. As discussed in the section on elbow injuries, a light grip pressure is best and will decrease both elbow and wrist injuries.

Carpal Tunnel Syndrome

Carpal tunnel syndrome (CTS) is a popular diagnosis in the lay press these days. It's mentioned and written about a lot in the newspapers. The incidence of this problem seems to be on the increase.

CTS occurs when the median nerve is compressed at the wrist by a thickened ligament that crosses over the nerve. The symptoms are pain in the wrist and, occasionally, in the fingers, with numbness in the thumb, index, and long fingers being common. Patients with CTS will often be awakened at night by the numbness and discomfort in their hands.

However, the pain and numbness in the hand can be caused by pressure on the nerves of the arm at any point from the neck to the wrist; it's not always caused by CTS. It has other numerous causes, too. The syndrome commonly occurs during pregnancy and is associated with rheumatoid arthritis and several hormonal problems.

CTS is often considered to be caused by repetitive overuse of the wrist and hands. In our computer society, continued hours of keyboarding is blamed for the CTS epidemic. It's unclear whether CTS is work-related or whether it's due to overuse. This issue is hotly debated and highly controversial.

Ken Venturi's career was eventually ended by CTS, and he had several wrist surgeries. However, I don't see a lot of CTS in golfers. I certainly see less CTS in golfers than I do in nongolfers, in particular, in patients working at repetitive jobs. I can only hypothesize that golf somehow is "carpal tunnel protective." I suspect that the exercise golf brings to the hand and the wrist somehow strengthens that area and, therefore, decreases the incidence of CTS in golfers.

If you do get CTS, however, there are numerous things that can be done, and surgery isn't the only option. Medical treatment of CTS begins with non-steroidal anti-inflammatory medication (NSAIDs). Most patients will also benefit from a wrist splint to place the wrist at rest and decrease inflammation about the nerve. As one recovers from CTS, however, exercise to regain mobility and strength about the wrist and hand is important, and again, hand therapists often work with CTS patients. Another treatment that has had some success is the use of vitamin B_6 as a diet supplement. The success rate is not uniform, but it's supported in the medical literature as a possible treatment.

Injecting the wrist area with cortisone may also decrease inflammation about the median nerve and help resolve the problem. However, because of the risk of tendon rupture, such an injection should rarely, if ever, be repeated. If none of these work, surgery is a last option.

If you elect surgery, it can be performed on an outpatient basis and is usually now done under local or a regional anesthesia. In this surgery, a small incision on the palm side of the wrist is made, and the ligament overlying and compressing the nerve is released. The surgery can also now be done via a method similar to arthroscopic surgery with several small incisions. This method carries a slightly greater risk of complications, however, and only certain surgeons are using this technique as a result. Recovery from carpal tunnel surgery usually takes several weeks, but results are quite good.

Wrist Ligament Injuries

Golfers get a ligament injury to the thumb termed a *gamekeeper's thumb*. The name is derived from nineteenth-century England, when gamekeepers killed chickens by wringing their heads and twisting them off with their thumb. It was a common injury from that torturous exercise. Today, it's most commonly seen among skiers, golfers, and basketball players.

In a gamekeeper's thumb, the ligaments at the base near the index finger are torn or ruptured. Golfers usually sustain this injury from a single, traumatic shot, such as taking a huge divot, or hitting an unseen rock or tree root. Among the professionals, Lee Trevino has had difficulty with this problem, and he eventually underwent a fairly complicated surgery that required taking a tendon from his wrist to reconstruct the ligament.

Former Massachusetts and New England Amateur Champion Bobby Caprera played on the golf team with me at Duke University. He might have become a professional but for this problem. He hurt his thumb playing basketball, had problems for years with it, and eventually came to surgery. Caprera managed to play by taping his thumb from just below his wrist to almost the tip of the thumb. This bandage helped him maintain control of the club at the top of his backswing, although occasionally he would hurt the area and drop the club before starting down. He did not do it for gamesmanship!

You may be able to play by trying to tape the thumb as just described. Another suggestion that would probably help is a grip change. If you have a "long thumb" grip, your thumb will be under high stress during your swing. You should probably talk to your professional and consider changing your grip to a "short thumb" on the left hand.

Gamekeeper's thumb occasionally requires surgery, but not always—cast treatment can be used in certain cases. The decision whether or not to operate is very difficult and must be individualized. The most important thing for a golfer to do when he or she sustains a single trauma on the index finger side of the thumb is to seek out an orthopaedist early and get treated. Either cast treatment or surgery works well if started early. Late treatment is far less successful.

Hand and Wrist Tendinitis

Golfers will also often develop tendinitis in their hands, wrists, and fingers. A common problem that is seen in golfers and in nongolfers is called a trigger finger. In a classic trigger finger, it's difficult to bend the finger and after bending, it becomes locked and cannot be straightened without pain. Unless you have a systemic disease like rheumatoid arthritis or gout, the underlying cause of trigger fingers is unknown. It can affect any of the fingers. I include the problem under tendinitis because, technically, it's called *stenosing tenosynovitis*, although every orthopaedist I know simply calls it a trigger finger. We can only be so verbose!

The mechanical cause of trigger finger, however, is known. It's a thickening or nodule formation on one of the flexor tendons in your palm. The tendons are covered by a thin sheath with gaps in it, and in a trigger finger, the nodule gets trapped between the gaps in this sheath. You can't flex the finger because the sheath won't allow the nodule to pass under it. Once you force the finger into flexion, the nodule is often trapped in one of the gaps in the sheath.

If the trigger finger isn't a significant problem, you can simply elect to ignore it, and live with it. It's not life threatening, and for some people it's simply a nuisance. For others, however, it's more troublesome. If so, you have two options for treatment, but you need to visit either an orthopaedic surgeon or a hand surgeon. The first option is nonoperative and consists of a steroid or cortisone injection into the tendon sheath. This procedure is often successful, and if it isn't, some physicians recommend a second injection.

Your second option is surgery, which can be done under local anesthesia on an outpatient basis. An incision is made in your palm, and the restricting sheath is released slightly to allow the nodule to pass under it more easily. You could probably be back playing in a few weeks.

If you have trigger finger, I can't really recommend any specific golf-related adjustments to help you play better. I doubt it will bother most golfers much, as they can surely grip the club. It is ungripping that may be difficult.

Golfers will very commonly develop tendinitis at the base of the thumb. This tendinitis, called *DeQuervain's tenosynovitis,* usually hurts on the side of the wrist just below the thumb. It can be very painful and take a long time to overcome.

Nobody knows exactly what causes DeQuervain's disease. It may be aggravated a bit by playing because of the jarring effects of taking divots or ball impact. I see a lot of golfers with this problem, and virtually all of them involve the left hand of right-handed golfers (or vice versa).

Treatment for DeQuervain's usually involves some rest to the injured area. Orthopaedists often treat the problem by putting the wrist and thumb in a small splint or brace to rest the inflamed tendons. Other treatments include taking anti-inflammatory medicine by mouth or getting a shot of cortisone around the injured tendons. Finally, if all else fails, a simple surgical procedure can be done that releases a tight sheath around the tendons and often effects a cure.

About playing golf with thumb tendinitis: It may be difficult. Certainly during the most painful periods, you will need to back off from playing as often and probably from practicing much. In addition, sweeping the ball with your irons and avoiding taking a divot may be helpful. If your partners will allow it, teeing the ball on all shots may allow you to play when you otherwise couldn't.

Technically, playing with a wrist or thumb splint is illegal. (The splint acts as a wrist brace—it's one reason you don't see golfers using wrist braces as bowlers do.) In friendly matches, you could probably play with a splint, although it would have to be fairly light and flexible to allow you to swing. What is legal and may help as much is taping your thumb and wrist, similar to what a trainer would do and similar to what we described earlier for a gamekeeper's thumb. A good tape job will provide as much support as a lightweight splint and should be very helpful while trying to play with DeQuervain's.

Hand Fractures and Injuries Specific to Golfers

The hamate bone is a small bone at the base of the wrist on the small finger side. It consists of a relatively larger section along with a smaller, protruding section, termed the "hook of the hamate," which is closer to the skin on the palm. The hamate is located just beyond the wrist crease in line with the little and ring fingers. This bone is very rarely injured.

However, when it is injured, that injury invariably occurs to a golfer, a tennis player, or a baseball player. The typical player that gets this injury is a professional or a low-handicap amateur who practices and plays a lot. This bone is the one John Cook broke and was not diagnosed for almost two years. It's also the injury that eventually ended Roger Maris's baseball career.

The reason for injury during these sports is that the hook of the hamate underlies the thick, muscular pad on the side of the palm opposite the thumb—technically termed the *hypothenar eminence*—and this pad is critical in gripping a golf club, tennis racket, or baseball bat. The shock of impact is transmitted directly to the hypothenar eminence of the left hand in a right-handed player. Practicing a lot leads occasionally to fractures of the this bone, which act like stress fractures. You usually don't notice a single injury that caused it. It simply comes from the stress of practicing a lot.

Because I see a lot of golfers, I diagnose about four or five of these injuries each year, which is a lot for one orthopaedic surgeon. The key to a diagnosis is being suspicious, because doctors who don't see many golfers or athletes will not suspect this rare injury. The diagnosis is difficult to make even on plain x-rays, and, in fact, the fracture can almost never be seen on a plain x-ray. The suspicious orthopaedist will order a special x-ray, either a CT (a "CAT scan"), or an MRI. Another type of x-ray, a bone scan, can also be used and will often help make the diagnosis.

If you have pain at the base of the hand or wrist on the small finger side, which does not resolve after three to four weeks, you should definitely seek out an orthopaedic or hand surgeon. I suggest mentioning that you are a golfer and that you have heard of this fracture and are concerned about it. Again, the fracture must be suspected, or else the proper studies will not be ordered.

If you have a hook of the hamate fracture, the treatment is usually surgery. The fracture rarely responds well to cast treatment, although I have had some success with a few patients treated this way. The fractured bone is very small, and the treatment is simply to remove the broken portion—no long-term deficit results from excising the broken fragment.

I have now performed this surgery on several professional golfers as well as on several low-handicap competitive amateur players. All have returned to their previous level of competition. Thus if suspected and diagnosed properly, this problem is highly treatable.

One tip may be helpful to prevent this problem—and golf glove manufacturers should probably start using it. After treating professsionals with this problem, I recommend they buy and play with bicycle gloves. These are half gloves in the older style of golf gloves, but they are padded on the palm, including over the area of the hook of the hamate bone. If you have had this problem or have pain in this area without having a fracture, try bicycle gloves while playing. The padding may help you.

What about blistering? Unfortunately, golfers who play or practice a lot will frequently develop blisters.

Blisters are usually a sign of movement. During the swing, the grip is moving slightly and rubbing the hand in such a way that, done repetitively, it causes a blister. The best treatment is probably a golf lesson to check for hand motion during the swing. You may be gripping and then regripping the club during the swing.

The lesson will likely consist of the following advice: The best treatment is to take your normal golf grip, remembering not to grip too tightly. After taking the grip, try to swing and to be conscious of your grip on the club. Try to maintain a constant grip pressure throughout the swing—not loosening your hands or tightening. You'll also likely become aware of any time that you are loosening or moving your grip.

Golfers who practice long hours will occasionally develop blisters simply from overuse. An excellent treatment for the cracking and drying that occurs from a blister is Nupercainal ointment. This over-the-counter ointment is usually used for hemorrhoids, but it softens blisters and has some medicinal properties that seem to heal them quickly. Apply some Nupercainal to your blisters, add a Band-Aid or two, and you can probably keep on playing and swinging. If the blister is on a finger, wrap some adhesive tape completely around the finger, over the Band-Aid, to keep it from slipping out of place.

Golfers who wear a glove and develop blisters on their glove hand should also check the size of the glove. It may be too large and move during your swing, causing the blister. Gloves should fit snugly. Alternately, try playing without a glove for a while, and see if that relieves the problem.

Another piece of equipment to check is your grips. Grips should be cleaned periodically, but few amateur players bother with this, and few golf shops have the time to clean off every grip for all the members. If your grips have not been cleaned in this decade or so, clean them carefully with soap and water. Be sure to clean the grips after playing because they will take at least overnight to dry adequately. If your grips are really worn out, another alternative is to replace them with new ones, which may help your blistering problem as well.

Preventing Hand and Wrist Injuries

Prevention of hand and wrist injuries begins with strengthening the muscles and tendons around the wrist. Strong hands are also helpful to improve your golf game. A certain degree of pressure is necessary to control the club during the swing. But if a player's hands are weak, the pressure needed to control the club is often a large percentage of the player's hand strength. This weakness causes tenseness in the arms and loss of motion at the wrists, which can inhibit the swing. Strong hands, wrists, and forearms allow a player to grip the club firmly but without exerting excess tension in those muscles, thereby freeing up the swing.

The best exercise for strengthening your hands or wrists for golf, other than hitting a lot of golf balls, is simply to squeeze a rubber ball or tennis ball continually. This exercise is used by many pro golfers and tennis players.

There are multiple other excellent exercises to strengthen the hands and wrists. We discussed some of them in the chapter on exercises for golf. Basically, weight training exercises that may help include wrist curls, reverse wrist curls, and using a wrist roller (although the last may be tough on the elbows or shoulders).

There are numerous other hand exercisers that involve various permutations of squeezing the hand and making a fist against resistance. Most of these are adequate and helpful, and I would definitely recommend a golfer with hand or wrist problems get one of these or simply start squeezing a rubber ball or tennis ball. The nice thing about this exercise for weekend golfers is that it can usually be done in the quiet of an office. When I played on the tour, I drove to most sites, and I always squeezed a rubber ball during the long drives. It helped strengthen my forearms and wrists a lot.

Your hands are your most important connection to the golf club. They transmit all the power of the golf swing, and they control the golf club, allowing you to control your golf ball. Take care of your hands, and they will take care of your golf game.

9

Lower Extremities

Golfers don't injure their legs as often as their other body parts, although it happens. In addition, many of you have lower-extremity ailments that stem from other sources. There are several things that can be done to overcome these problems or to prevent their occurrence, starting with the stance.

Which Stance and How Wide?

There are several ways to stand to the ball, all acceptable according to your body and swing type. A square stance is one in which a line drawn across both toes would be parallel to your target line. A closed stance (for right-handers) would point to the right of the target line, whereas an open stance would point to the left of the target line (again for right-handed players).

Classic teaching emphasizes the need to use a square stance or even a slightly open stance, but be aware that this stance is for the good player in good condition. However, many older players and players with shoulder, back, hip, and leg problems or less flexibility should consider using a closed stance because these problems make it difficult to make a big turn on the backswing. The closed stance does a big turn for you. On the backswing, it gets the back turned farther away from the target; on the forward swing, it lets you swing more from the inside, which is desirable. Leave the open stance to players with no back or leg problems and excellent flexibility.

In addition, as you lose flexibility as you get older or if you have back or leg problems, you need to narrow your stance a bit—bring your feet closer together. A wider stance restricts the hip turn. The more that is restricted, the more the turn will have to be made with the upper body. Turning the upper body a lot against a minimal hip turn places a great deal of stress on the lower back and can lead to injury.

A narrow stance, on the other hand, allows you to turn your hips more easily. This will take stress off the lower back and lower extremities while still allowing you to turn your upper body freely. One drill that is often used by teaching professionals is to have players hit balls with their feet together. This encourages good balance and promotes a bigger upper body turn while not restricting the hip turn. It's a drill all older golfers or golfers with back and leg problems should try, and the basic premise of the narrower stance should become a part of your golf philosophy.

When taking this narrow, slightly closed stance, you should consider where the ball should be played. Classic teaching again says that the "best" position is off the left toe or the inside of the left heel for the driver shot or slightly farther back toward the center of your stance for the irons. This position is fine for young and athletic individuals who have a well-honed swing and can make a strong, athletic weight shift toward the target during the downswing. But if you have back or lower-extremity problems, this weight shift gets more difficult. You may benefit from keeping the ball farther back in the stance, so you can hit it squarely without having to shift your weight dramatically to the left.

How far away from your body should the ball be placed at address? The closer the better to minimize strain on your back and, subsequently, the legs. The farther away from your body the ball is placed, the more you will have to bend from the waist to address it properly. This places more strain on the back and legs. Bring the ball in as close as you feel comfortable doing. This ball position causes you to stand up a bit straighter, which makes your swing plane a bit flatter. Thus your back rotates on a flatter plane, which greatly decreases the pressure on the back and lower extremities. Bending a lot and then turning the back loads it a great deal.

Finally, you should consider the position of your feet at address. In his classic book, *Five Lessons: The Modern Fundamentals of Golf*, Ben Hogan makes the statement that the feet should be positioned with the right foot perpendicular to the target line and the left foot set "a quarter turn" or $22^{1}/_{2}°$ (for right-handed golfers) to the left. That's pretty precise, as Hogan was, but you get the idea. This approximate foot position may be ideal for players with normal flexibility in their hips, knees, and ankles, and I would never advise against it.

However, not everybody has normal flexibility in the lower extremities. If that's your situation, you may not be able to achieve those foot positions without placing undue stress on your legs. This may, in particular, affect you if you try to turn the left foot out as Hogan prescribes. Many people walk with their toes turned in—pigeon-toed. In that case, turning out your left foot will be very stressful on your knees, in particular. You can solve this problem by squaring your left foot more or by turning your whole body a bit more toward the target—in other words, play with more of an open stance. That may seem contradictory to the advice I gave you earlier, but you should experiment to find the stance and address position that best accommodates your particular problem.

Hip Problems among Golfers

Bursitis of the hip is a common problem among adults. Bursitis usually causes pain on the outside of the hip, near the prominent bone located there. This prominence is very close to the skin and is referred to as the *greater trochanter*. Directly overlying the greater trochanter is a bursa, which can become inflamed.

A bursa, found in many areas of the body, is a sac that contains a small amount of fluid, unless it's grossly inflamed, in which case it swells with a lot of fluid. The purpose of a bursa is lubrication. In the hip, several large muscles and tendons attach to the greater trochanter, and they could become irritated, but the bursa serves as a protector. Unfortunately, it too can become inflamed on occasion.

Golf swings put this area at risk because of the hip turn, in which the tendons and bursa often will slide over the edge of the greater trochanter. When this action happens continually, bursitis can result.

The best swing modification is to increase your hip turn. As I've indicated earlier, this may sound unusual, but the hip turn actually takes stress off the hips by increasing the rotation of the lower back. This will prevent sliding of the bursa at the hip and take stress off the area.

The medical treatment for hip bursitis usually begins with rest to decrease the irritation. You may have to lay off golf awhile. Icing the area of inflammation also will help, usually. Your doctor also will likely prescribe some anti-inflammatory medications, such as aspirin, ibuprofen, or possibly a prescription medicine. These should be taken with care by any person with ulcers or a history of stomach irritation.

Cortisone shots are controversial in most inflammatory processes in the body. However, a cortisone injection to the greater trochanter is often almost curative and is used quite often by orthopaedists. It's one affliction where little risk exists from the injection. If you're not responding to rest, medication, and icing, a cortisone injection may help you. Surgery is almost never required for this problem.

Hip arthritis is a major problem in older golfers, although it may not be related in any way to playing the game. It's simply a result of the aging process.

If hip arthritis advances far enough, it may require a hip replacement to alleviate the symptoms. Hip replacements will be discussed in detail in the chapter "Special Health Problems."

The medical treatment for hip arthritis usually involves mild medicines to decrease inflammation in the hip joint. Many of these are now available as over-the-counter medicines.

An excellent treatment for hip arthritis involves simply using a cane. It's not glamorous, but a cane often will allow a patient to take stress off the painful hip. It should be used in the hand opposite the painful hip, that is, the left hand for a painful right hip and vice versa.

Now, you might think that you don't want to bother with a cane while playing, but think again. You carry fourteen canes in your golf bag. If you have hip arthritis, simply take a club, turn it upside down, grasp the club head with your hand, and use the grip as the end of the cane. Use a club as a cane, and you'll be able to play more comfortably.

Swing adjustments also may help. In this case, I would recommend shortening your swing and using a small hip turn. The larger hip turn that I recommend for most conditions will increase rotation at the hips and likely will hurt. The small hip turn will decrease rotation at the hips. And I would recommend, as I often do, that golfers with hip arthritis learn to play on their toes. By coming up on your left toe at the top of the backswing and finishing well up on your right toe, less stress will be imparted to the hips.

Golfer's Knee Injuries

Probably the most-publicized injury in sports during the 1990s is a tear of the anterior cruciate ligament (ACL) of the knee. Golfers will very rarely tear an ACL, although I've seen it happen in golf cart injuries in which the golfer didn't keep his feet inside the cart and caught his foot on a retaining fence. However, many golfers will suffer an ACL tear because of a ligament tear when they were younger. Because surgery to reconstruct the ACL was only popularized in the mid-1970s, many older golfers who sustained this injury before then have lived and played golf without an anterior cruciate ligament for some time.

You can play golf without an anterior cruciate ligament, although you may have some episodes of "catching" in your knee—it feels like your knee is slipping out of place. Older golfers may benefit from a brace that is prescribed by an orthopaedic surgeon specifically to stabilize a knee without an ACL. Again, playing on your toes will benefit you and prevent periods of instability associated with an absent ACL.

Should older golfers consider surgery to reconstruct an anterior cruciate ligament? Possibly, but it should be discussed in detail with an orthopaedic surgeon. We know that people without an ACL tend to develop cartilage tears in their knees with high frequency. In addition, we know that loss of this cartilage will lead to degenerative arthritis as one ages. Thus, loss of the ACL is thought to be a predisposing factor to knee arthritis. It may be that you have already developed arthritis in your knee and this may keep you from being a candidate for reconstructive surgery.

If you tear your ACL in high school or college, you have a long time to develop arthritis, assuming you don't participate in sports that involve cutting a lot and putting a lot of stress on the knee. Thus, most modern orthopaedists recommend that almost all teenagers or individuals in their early twenties undergo a reconstructive procedure for this injury.

Our studies of ACL reconstruction are short term because we have only been doing the surgery for about fifteen years, but it appears that well-done reconstructions last and provide some immunity against cartilage tears. Thus, although we don't have long-term followup, we think people will get less knee arthritis after an ACL reconstruction. So golfers probably should give strong consideration to having the operation. You must understand, however, that you will be rehabilitating this knee for up to a year, and your effort at rehab is probably the strongest determining factor in how good the results will be.

Golfers don't often tear knee ligaments, but they often tear the knee cartilage, which is one of the two menisci in your knee. There are two types of knee cartilage: the articular cartilage, which covers the end of the bone; and the meniscus, which is sometimes referred to as the floating cartilage. This is often torn with twisting maneuvers when the knee is under some force; for example, being hit when playing football or being twisted at the end of a golf swing.

The meniscus usually does not heal by itself. However, not all torn menisci require surgery. A small tear may become asymptomatic. If the tear is small enough, you may be able to live with it and suffer only occasional discomfort. It's possible that the tear could get larger, and if that happens, you may then require surgery. Signs that the tear is very large are a grossly swollen knee, a knee locked in a position that can be neither straightened fully or bent all the way, and continued catching and popping within in the knee, especially during weight-bearing occasions.

If you're not currently having any of those symptoms, it's probably acceptable to try to get along without surgery. Surgery on torn knee cartilages these days is done almost exclusively with an arthroscope. In this type of surgery, no large incision is made in the knee. Arthroscopic surgery consists of placing a scope into an arthrus, or joint; hence, arthroscope. The arthroscope measures about three to six millimeters in diameter, and instruments of corresponding diameter allow the surgery to be done through several small incisions measuring no more than one centimeter in diameter.

The surgeon doesn't actually look into the joint, nor does he even look at the patient's body very often. After the arthroscope is introduced, it's connected to a television camera, and the surgeon looks into the body through a television screen. After the diagnosis is confirmed, arthroscopic instruments are inserted through a second small incision to perform surgery. The procedure is actually very similar to playing a video game.

Difficult as it may seem to believe, a surgeon can see more of a joint through an arthroscope than he can see through many types of open surgery. The surgical procedures that can be done are a bit limited, however. The most common arthroscopic procedures are done on the knee and include excision or repair of cartilage, or meniscal, tears, and assisted-repair of the anterior cruciate ligament. In the shoulder, cartilage, or labral, tears can be excised and trimmed, bone spurs can be removed, and stabilizing procedures can even be done now for dislocating shoulders. Arthroscopy is now also performed on the ankle, wrist, and elbow, though with less frequency.

For knee cartilage tears, arthroscopy is used to either shave the torn portion of the cartilage or, in younger patients with large tears, repair the tear with sutures. This may require a slightly larger incision made on the side of the knee.

Arthroscopy is done almost exclusively on an out-patient basis. Many surgeons perform the procedure using local anesthesia, which greatly reduces the risk of the surgery. Recovery after meniscus surgery with an arthroscope is relatively rapid. Most people have some pain after the surgery but can walk within a day or two. Often they are back to normal in a few weeks.

Because of the twisting motions required during a golf swing, golf is an excellent trial to see if you can get along without the surgery. There's no harm in trying to play golf with a torn meniscus. If you can tolerate the twisting of the swing, you'll probably be able to avoid surgery. If you can't play with this injury, no swing modifications will help much. You should consider having the arthroscopic procedure.

Some individuals also will dislocate their kneecaps, although rarely while playing golf. However, if you have had knee dislocations, they often become recurrent, and the kneecap may go partially out of joint during a golf swing. The left kneecap (patella) is at risk to dislocate at the top of the backswing of a right-handed golfer, whereas the right kneecap can dislocate during the follow-through.

Dislocation occurs because of the turning of the hips during the backswing. The hips turn, but the feet are relatively planted. Thus, a torque is applied to the knees, and if your kneecaps have an inclination to do so, they may dislocate or partially dislocate.

One solution is to make some swing modifications. Again, you should swing without keeping your feet planted, rising on your left toe at the top of your backswing (if you are right-handed), and up on your right toe near impact and into your follow-through. Second, you should also learn to decrease your hip turn a bit especially if it's your lead knee that's bothering you. By decreasing your hip turn, you'll decrease the twisting motion that is applied to that knee.

The treatment for a subluxating or dislocating kneecap initially begins with therapy and rehabilitation exercises. Treatment is aimed at strengthening certain muscles of the thigh and stretching out other muscles. Dislocated kneecaps are most common in adolescent women, for certain biomechanical reasons related to the changing shape of a female's body at that age. In recurrent cases that do not respond to therapy and rehab, surgery is occasionally necessary.

Foot and Ankle Problems

The most common of these injuries is a sprained ankle, which occurs often while playing golf and walking on uneven ground. Virtually all ankle sprains are tears of the lateral ligaments on the outside of your ankle. It's very rare to tear the inner (medial) ligaments. Unfortunately, in a good golf swing, you should roll over onto the outside of your lead foot and ankle during your follow-through. This motion is exactly the one that caused your ankle sprain, although that occurred at a much higher speed and force. Thus, with every golf swing, you are stressing those torn ligaments and probably causing microtears in the ligament as it's trying to heal. This problem doesn't happen with the trailing ankle because very little stress is put on it during the backswing, and virtually no stress is incurred on the downswing and follow-through.

Golfers with acute ankle sprains will need to cut back on playing awhile. Practice is definitely out for two or three weeks. If your ankle swells a lot after playing, I'd recommend not playing again until the swelling subsides. It's not uncommon for several months after ankle sprains for your ankle to swell a bit after exercise. So for the next several months, icing after playing will prevent swelling and inflammation and decrease your pain. You could also try playing with your ankle taped, or you could use an orthotic called an AirCast. Either will protect your ankle a bit, although they both may restrict your follow-through. Thus you may not play as well until you fully recover from this injury.

If you sustain a target-side ankle sprain and feel you must play—the second-flight championship in your club tournament is really that important, isn't it?—you probably will benefit from turning your target-side foot out more (toward the target) at address. This will ease the pressure on the ankle on the follow-through.

Many individuals—golfers and others—develop troublesome pain in the base of the heel. This pain is often diagnosed as a bone spur, but the problem is more commonly an inflammation of the *plantar fascia*, the tough, tendon-like structure that runs from the heel to the balls of your feet. When it becomes inflamed, called *plantar fasciitis*, it usually hurts underneath the heel where the fascia attaches to the heel bone (calcaneus).

This condition is aggravated by tight heel cords, the tendons attaching to the calf muscles. Women often develop this problem because high-heeled shoes tighten the heel cords. After wearing high heels, the condition is aggravated by wearing flats, such as golf shoes.

Start the rehabilitation process by stretching your heel cord and calf muscle. To do this, stand about two feet from a wall and lean forward gradually with your heels staying flat on the floor. You should feel a stretch in the back of your calves. Another method is to stand on a step with only your toes, letting your weight push your heels down below the step to stretch the heel cord. Also, in the future, avoid high-heeled shoes.

While helping stretch your tight heel cords, you need to work on the preexisting inflammation by icing the area after it becomes painful and limiting activities while it is painful. Also, taking daily doses of aspirin or a stronger anti-inflammatory medicine is often helpful, provided you have no stomach or ulcer problems.

Various shoe inserts can be helpful in curing this condition. Some individuals obtain relief from an arch support, although this often is painful because it puts pressure directly over the inflamed area. A heel wedge can be placed on the medial (inside) side of the heel, often with good results. Both of these can be obtained at drugstores without a prescription. You should also take a good look at your golf shoes. They should be well padded and not old and worn out. Spikeless shoes may also take stress off the heel area.

In recalcitrant cases, the area can be injected with steroids. If all else fails, the fascia can be released surgically. You probably can avoid that, however, with stretching, ice, limiting your activity, appropriate shoe inserts, and aspirin. Besides, the surgery is not always successful, so avoid it if at all possible.

Severe pain on the outside of your left ankle just below the ankle bone can be a sign of tendinitis, which often occurs in golfers. This type is known as peroneal tendinitis—the tendons on the outside of the ankle are the peroneal tendons.

Peroneal tendinitis is not uncommon among golfers. Lee Trevino was once quoted as saying that all professional golfers had problems in this area at one time or another. The difficulty occurs near impact and into follow-through when the golfer rolls over onto the outside of his left (or lead) ankle. This position puts a significant stretch on the peroneal tendons. Excessive practice or play can place continued stress on these tendons, and they may become inflamed and develop tendinitis.

Treatment of tendinitis or soft-tissue inflammation in any area of the body can be easily recalled with a mnemonic known as R-I-C-E. This stands for R = rest, I = ice, C = compression, and E = elevation.

Rest, unfortunately, begins with eliminating the activity that causes the problem, in this case, golf. A short break from playing and practicing may be necessary. Other methods of rest may be necessary in extreme cases—an ankle brace or cast to limit use of the tendons and allow them a chance to heal might be described. This treatment is now slightly controversial and is used less commonly than previously. A serious discussion with your physician is in order before deciding on this treatment.

After you resume playing, the area may again become inflamed and swollen, which can lead to stiffness and prolonged rehabilitation. Ice should then be used to reduce the inflammation, but be careful not to use it for more than fifteen or twenty minutes at a time. Left on too long, ice can cause problems with nerves and the skin. Compression, usually with an elastic wrap or by taping, often helps reduce the swelling. Elevation of the area has the same effect.

When the tendinitis improves or resolves, rehabilitation is critical to prevent a recurrence of the injury. Your doctor or a physical therapist can recommend a program to strengthen the tendons and make them more flexible.

One move that may help a golfer play with this problem is to turn the lead foot more toward the target. This will reduce pressure on the foot because there will be less tendency to roll over onto the ankle during the follow-through.

10

Special Health Problems

Arthritis—Rheumatoid and Other Types

Arthritis is the term used to describe inflammation of a joint. There are many different types of arthritis. The most common is *osteoarthritis,* or degenerative arthritis, often called "wear-and-tear" or "old-age" arthritis. This type of arthritis is one in which a single joint usually gradually wears out. It often develops because of an old injury, such as an old football injury or perhaps an old fracture near a joint. In some cases, individuals will develop degenerative arthritis in several joints.

Rheumatoid arthritis is a disease that affects the entire body. This special type of arthritis is termed an *inflammatory arthropathy.* Other types of inflammatory arthropathies are *systemic lupus erythematosus* (lupus), *psoriatic arthritis,* and *anklyosing spondylitis.*

All these diseases share a common element and are termed *auto-immune diseases*. With auto-immune diseases, in some way, the body's immune system turns against itself and literally attacks certain areas of the body. Especially in rheumatoid arthritis, the most obvious destruction occurs to the joints. But in all inflammatory arthropathies, other organ systems can be involved. Treatment of inflammatory arthropathies is thus more difficult and is often handled by internists or rheumatologists. Orthopaedic surgeons usually become involved only when specific surgical problems develop.

Treatment of arthritis depends on the type of disease and its severity. Physical therapy is often used and can be critical in allowing patients to retain full range of motion in the involved joints. Heat and ice often help decrease symptoms. Certain medicines, especially in patients with gout, are remarkably successful in helping patients live with the diseases. Joint replacement surgery can bring excellent relief in patients with severe joint involvement.

Playing golf with arthritis is difficult. Actually, playing any sport with any form of arthritis is difficult, but it's very important that you do so. Individuals with arthritis need to stay as active as possible to avoid muscle deterioration and joint stiffness. The problem is that exercise is often painful. The trick is to balance mild, gentle exercise to maintain muscle and joint tone without overdoing and increasing the inflammation so that exercise becomes more painful.

The most important thing to remember with any arthritis is to warm up carefully before going out to play. You may need to wear some extra clothing, even on days that seem relatively warm. I'd also recommend loosening up those stiff, painful joints under a warm shower before you play, and ideally, it could be done in your club locker room. At the course, be certain to spend some time on the practice range first, building up with some short half shots, before proceeding to full swings. At least fifteen or twenty minutes should be spent on the practice tee before playing, which, in fact, is a good rule for all players.

Choosing your days to play is also important. Cool, rainy days are almost prohibitive for many individuals with arthritis. There are some valid scientific reasons this is so—it's not an old wives' tale. If you have arthritis and the day is very cool and rainy, you may need to decide how much today's golf game really means to you. If you decide to play, again, dress very warmly. You may want to carry a hand warmer with you as well.

Arthritis strikes the body's joints relatively selectively. The most involved joints tend to be the hips, the knees, and the hands. Many individuals with hip and knee arthritis walk with a cane to take pressure off the joints. Some golfers prefer not to, but as I said in the last chapter, you're carrying fourteen "canes" with you. You can ease your arthritic pain somewhat by turning a short iron upside down, gripping the club head with your hand, and using the upside-down club as a pseudo-cane. It will take some pressure off the affected joints.

Generally, individuals with hip arthritis will benefit from using a cane or the upside-down club in the hand opposite the painful hip, while knee arthritis patients derive more benefit if the cane is on the same side as the painful knee.

The best way to play with arthritis in your hands is by using oversized grips. Several of the grip manufacturers make special grips for individuals with arthritic hands. In addition, your golf pro or a club shop can specially build up your grips so that they are much thicker than normal. Finally, most pro shops carry special grip gauze that can be wrapped around the grips. This gauze is usually used on putters, but it can be placed on any grip and will add even more thickness and padding to the grip.

Individuals with significant arthritic pain in their hands will benefit from golf grips built up almost to the size of a tennis grip. In addition to making it easier to get your hands closed on the club, the large-sized grip also will provide padding to absorb the shock and sting of the impact.

It often happens that your arthritis is so severe that you need more than simple medical treatment to continue functioning. Today's orthopaedic surgeon commonly replaces knee joints and hip joints. Other joints, notably the shoulder, also can be replaced, but this is done less often. Can you play golf with these artificial joints? Absolutely.

Total hip replacement was the first truly common form of artificial joint replacement. The procedure was pioneered in the 1950s in Great Britain by Sir John Charnley. For his efforts, Charnley was knighted and nominated for the Nobel prize in medicine, although he never received it.

There can be problems with total hip replacements, and they won't last forever. We expect them to last about ten to fifteen years before they loosen and become painful again. Almost all orthopaedic surgeons allow their patients with artificial hip joints to play golf, and most golfers have few problems with them.

If your orthopaedic surgeon thinks you are a candidate for hip replacement, your desire to continue playing golf should not stop you. In fact, you likely will have less pain after the surgery and may be able to play much better. Many older golfers elect to have the surgery because it allows them to continue playing golf.

Doctors do not unanimously agree about playing golf with a total knee replacement, and some orthopaedists feel that it's not wise to play golf with an artificial knee joint. The knee is basically a hinge joint—it bends back and forth. An artificial knee (known as a total knee replacement or TKR to orthopaedists) also bends back and forth very well. But the human knee is more complicated than a pure hinge and also rotates, a motion that is controlled by various ligaments. Artificial knees don't tolerate rotation well.

The problem with golf and knee replacements is that the sport demands a turning or twisting of the body, therefore putting a great deal of stress on the knee and forcing it to rotate slightly. A knee replacement will not tolerate this nearly as well as a normal knee. The danger is that by playing too much golf, the stress will cause the artificial knee to loosen from its connection to bone.

Still, most orthopaedic surgeons allow their patients to continue playing after knee replacement surgery, and there have been few reported problems related to golf. In certain cases, there may be excessive bone loss that may put the patient at high risk playing golf. You could discuss this problem with your orthopaedic surgeon.

For any golfer with a total joint replacement, I'd make the following recommendations to help take pressure off the artificial joint and also prevent any disastrous complications that might occur if you accidentally fall:

- I wouldn't advise playing golf in wet weather—slipping and falling while making a swing or walking on a slope could be disastrous. In addition, bad weather still may cause you to have some minor aches and pains about the joint replacement.

- The golfer-patient may be able to play better without golf spikes—if the feet are not quite as stationary, they can turn a bit during the swing and take the stress off the knee or hip. The golfer-patient must be cautioned, however, that the chance of slipping and falling without spikes is slightly increased, so he or she needs to be very careful to avoid any potential slipping and falling. Again, playing in wet weather should be avoided!

- Any golfer with a joint replacement should learn to play more on the toes. Golfers with artificial joints should pay no attention to the articles and lessons from golf professionals who tell them not to raise up much on their toes. This style is for young, flexible golfers with normal joints. Swinging flat-footed places a lot of stress on the joint replacement. On the backswing, the left heel should come off the ground, and on the forward swing, the right heel should come off the ground.

- Golfers with total hip replacements should learn to play with a bigger hip turn. This advice may sound paradoxical, but the hip turn is really done by the lower back, by the trunk muscles. By turning the trunk more, the muscles about the hip are stretched less and take stress off the hip replacement. This turn must be accompanied by playing on the toes, however, or the stress of the trunk rotation will be transmitted to either the hip or knee.

As I mentioned, many older golfers are hoping to play a lot of golf, and the prospect of not being able to do so because of a painful hip or knee is daunting, at best. Dr. Clement Sledge, renowned joint replacement surgeon, has said that one of the questions most frequently asked by his patients is whether they will be able to play golf after the surgery.

The following quote from Dr. Lester Borden, a prominent orthopaedic surgeon and a member of The Hip Society, seems a most appropriate comment:

From a philosophical standpoint, I am a firm believer in helping individuals with arthritis to enjoy a good quality of life. I know how important golf is to individuals of all ages from both a social and competitive point of view. My experience has been gratifying with these individuals. It can be quite depressing for an individual facing retirement to know that he will have to give up a sport which he can finally play when he wishes and which he loves. Total joint arthroplasty [replacement] has allowed the vast majority of these

*individuals to continue the sport during their
retirement years and has clearly improved
their quality of living. Isn't that what it is
all about?*

Diabetes

Diabetes is a debilitating disease that receives almost
no attention from the media around the world but
affects the lives of millions of individuals. The basic
problem with diabetes is a lack of insulin in the body,
which is normally produced by the pancreas, a gland in
the abdomen. In some cases, the pancreas produces
adequate amounts of insulin, but the body doesn't
respond to it. The result is that the normal level of
blood sugar is not adequately controlled.

Diabetics develop multiple health problems. The
most life-threatening problem is heart disease. Diabetes causes development of atherosclerosis, or a
clogging of the arteries, which often manifests itself
in decreased blood flow to the heart. It also can cause
decreased blood flow in the legs, and diabetics often
develop circulatory problems in their legs.

The three significant health problems that are not
life threatening but affect many diabetics are known to
doctors as the *triopathy*. These are the development of
retinopathy (eye problems), *nephropathy* (decreased
kidney function), and *neuropathy* (decreased sensation
in the feet).

Treatment of diabetes was formerly always done by
insulin, once it was discovered. Now many diabetics
can be treated with oral medication to avoid the daily

injections. In addition, careful control of diet and weight is essential for all diabetics. Finally, pumps that automatically inject a certain amount of insulin continuously into the bloodstream are now available, although they are usually required in only the most severe cases.

Playing golf with diabetes is not only possible, but also highly beneficial. Almost all diabetics are now encouraged to stay active and exercise as much as possible. Current professional golfers Scott Verplank, Michelle McGann, and Mark Lye have diabetes and still manage to play professionally.

But diabetics must be careful while playing golf. Extreme swings in blood sugar can be dangerous and must be watched. Diabetics need to eat often while exercising. They should also consider monitoring their blood glucose during the round. If you check your own blood sugar with a special meter, as a precaution, you may wish to carry one in your golf bag.

Some diabetics probably should not exercise much, but these individuals are rare. Most doctors recommend that gentle aerobic exercise is very good for their diabetic patients. Golf is an almost ideal activity because it's both gentle and aerobic (assuming you walk). But diabetics with eye problems and kidney problems must check with their doctors to get approval for any exercise. In fact, all diabetics should check with their doctor before beginning any exercise regimen, including deciding to play a lot of golf.

Because diabetics may have decreased sensation in their feet and lower legs, proper footwear and clothing is essential. Diabetics must inspect their feet daily to be certain no wounds or cuts or scrapes have occurred.

Inspection is especially important after a round of golf because small sand pebbles or other sharp items may get in the golf shoes while playing. While individuals with normal sensation will feel this, diabetics may not. If a small cut or scrape is not recognized, it can get infected and may lead to a disastrous complication.

Because of decreased sensation, I would advise all diabetics to wear long pants while playing. The pant legs will protect the lower legs against any small scrapes or cuts that might occur while in the woods or in underbrush looking for golf balls. (If you never miss the fairway and never play with anybody who does, perhaps you get could away with shorts, but I wouldn't recommend it!)

Since diabetics shouldn't wear shorts, playing on hot days is especially dangerous for them. In fact, diabetics more than likely are better off not playing on exceptionally hot days. Diabetics frequently have mild, often unrecognized, heart disease, and the excess strain of hot weather may be dangerous. Playing in extreme weather conditions should only be done by those who have become inured to the heat by careful and gradual acclimatization.

Diabetics must watch their diet carefully while playing. They should always eat forty-five to sixty minutes before the golf round or shortly before going out to warm up. They should drink plenty of fluids to keep well hydrated, especially on a sunny, warm day. After the round, diabetics may see their blood glucose and their need for insulin decrease dramatically, so they should be careful about injecting the normal insulin dose. They may wish to discuss this insulin dose with the doctor and monitor the glucose carefully after every round.

During the golf game bring snacks such as fruits and raisins to help keep the blood sugar elevated. If you begin to feel faint or woozy on the course, sit down, drink some water, and begin eating some of the snacks immediately. However, you should avoid highly sweetened snacks such as candy or sugar colas. You may wish to carry some fruit juice with you in your golf bag. It could be life-saving.

If you are a diabetic, exercise can kill you if you overdo it. But careful, well-monitored aerobic exercise can prolong your life and greatly improve the quality of living. Golf is a perfect choice, so go for it!

Heart Problems

Almost all golfers with heart disease should be able to continue playing golf. In fact, playing golf may be good for a patient with cardiac disease. Remember that one of the mainstays of current treatment of heart disease is moderate exercise. It helps by lowering blood pressure and controlling weight, and it's also helpful in lowering cholesterol counts.

Golf has been studied for all these effects, and it's definitely a useful exercise for cardiac rehabilitation. However, the studies were done on individuals who walked the golf course. Riding in a golf cart will provide absolutely no benefit at all for your heart. Golf, if you walk while playing, is an excellent exercise because the game entails a walk of five to six miles spread over three to four hours—and I hope no more (see Figure 10–1).

I don't mean you should not approach the situation with some caution. You should discuss playing golf with your internist or cardiologist. You likely will be

Figure 10–1 Two golfers enjoying the best way to play golf and getting the most health benefit from the game—walking the course.

Courtesy Jim Moriarty/
Mr. Ed Ibarguen and
Ms. Jaime Koizumi

placed on certain medications, and you should take these under their guidance. Remember, some medications may have deleterious effects on the body during very hot weather. Heart patients also may not have sufficient cardiac reserves to play effectively in the heat, and hot days may simply have to be avoided. If you have heart problems and elect to play in hot weather, do so with extreme caution. See the section on playing in the heat, and follow all the advice. As stated in that section, very hot weather is one time that riding a cart may be the better part of valor.

Problems of Women Golfers

Women are physiologically different than men. You knew that, of course. But because of this difference, they have some unique problems and health considerations that don't affect men. Mainly, women are capable of bearing children, and they have menstrual periods. Women's menstrual periods can cause difficulty with competitive play. If the periods cause severe discomfort, most women simply elect not to play on those days when it's a noncompetitive situation.

Women have won gold medals during all phases of the menstrual cycle. Large-scale studies of women during menses have shown minimal changes in neuromuscular coordination, with the only significant ones being a slight decrease in that coordination just before the onset of the period and a slight increase in coordination just after the onset. However, individually, these changes may vary, and different golfers will have different responses to different phases of the cycle, with possible changes in concentration and skill.

The most significant physical difficulties that women endure related to the menstrual period are cramping, low back pain, and breast tenderness. To avoid these problems and their possible deleterious effects on physical skills during competition, start some anti-inflammatory medicines (such as aspirin, ibuprofen, naprosyn) twenty-four hours before the onset of menses and continue until about twenty-four hours after. This regimen will only work well in women whose periods are very regular.

You can play golf during pregnancy. At the 1995 U.S. Women's Open, professional player Dawn Coe-Jones finished four rounds while nearly six months pregnant.

Obstetricians tell their patients that aerobic exercise is not only acceptable during pregnancy, but also preferable. Any aerobic exercise you did before pregnancy can be continued safely during pregnancy, even up to the last few days before delivery. The last few weeks may be difficult, depending on your comfort level, but there's no danger to the baby or you if you are able to play.

There are a few exceptions. Some women have difficult pregnancies and are at risk for premature delivery, extreme high blood pressure, and a tendency toward diabetes during pregnancy. If you fall in these categories, your obstetrician will probably ask you to restrict your activity somewhat. You should always check with your obstetrician before beginning any exercise during pregnancy.

As I've already said, golf qualifies as an aerobic activity, especially if you are walking the course, and should be an excellent exercise during pregnancy. Again, riding a golf cart may be jarring to you and junior if the ride is at all bumpy. You may have to avoid golf carts, which makes the game a much better exercise.

Now, can you play as well as you did before being pregnant? Certainly you can during the first few months, until you can gain some weight. However, by the last trimester (last three months), most women have gained twenty to twenty-five pounds. Some of this weight is the baby, and some is from fluid that is due to hormonal changes. This fluid is being used to support the fetus during pregnancy and prepare the mother for nursing the infant. A large number of women develop back and pelvic pain during pregnancy because of this weight gain—and because of the position of the weight. If pain occurs, you may have some problems playing golf, which also can exacerbate back problems.

Treatment of this problem is usually twofold. First, limit your weight gain during pregnancy to the acceptable limits your obstetrician recommends. Second, exercises to strengthen the abdominal muscles and to keep the back flat can help. A strong back keeps the weight of the baby from moving too far forward and keeps it supported by the pelvic bones. The main exercise to strengthen the back is to lie flat on your back with your knees bent and your hips flexed. If you place your hand under your back, you will feel a space between your back and the floor. You need to flatten out this space by using your stomach muscles to push your back against the floor (or your hand—it's a good reminder to keep it there). Doing this exercise for ten to twenty repetitions every day during pregnancy should help keep your back strong and allow you to play golf.

The last major problem common among women is actually more applicable to older women—osteoporosis. Older men also can develop osteoporosis, but it's much more common among women.

Osteoporosis is a thinning or weakening of the bone, and it occurs as individuals get older. It's a prime cause of hip fractures and spinal compression fractures in the elderly that cause the so-called dowager's hump. There are many, many causes, but most individuals have what we call idiopathic osteoporosis, which means we're not really sure what causes it. We do know the risk factors very well, however. You are at high risk to develop osteoporosis if you are white, female, post-menopausal, thin, don't exercise, smoke, drink caffeine drinks and alcohol excessively, or take certain anti-seizure medications.

There is little you can do about being white or female, but if you're concerned about osteoporosis, you should try some lifestyle modifications to eliminate the other risk factors just mentioned. Avoid smoking and drinking alcohol or caffeine drinks (I didn't say this would be fun), and get regular, moderate exercise. In addition, the rate of bone loss can be slowed by using calcium and vitamin D supplements in your diet. I would recommend all women over forty (and probably all men also) supplement their diets so that they take in one thousand to fifteen hundred milligrams of calcium and four hundred units of vitamin D per day. The American diet usually doesn't supply more than a small portion of those nutrients. You can drink milk or other dairy products, but few adults drink six glasses of milk or eat eight pieces of cheese per day. If you don't, you need some supplementation.

Once women pass menopause, they are at very high risk of developing osteoporosis. In this case, many doctors recommend estrogen supplements to retard the loss of bone mass. There are, however, some risks with these, notably, increased risk of breast cancer. These should be discussed by you and your internist or gynecologist. Most of the risks can be lessened by adding another hormone, progesterone, to the estrogen supplement.

And yes, you can and should continue to play golf. Gentle forms of exercise are excellent to prevent continued bone loss. The exercise must be done in moderation, because exercise that is too vigorous can occasionally cause fractures. Gentle, aerobic exercise or low-intensity weightlifting are both helpful in maintaining bone mass. Walking a golf course is an excellent exercise and should be preferred by older women because of the many health benefits, not the least of which is the prevention of osteoporosis.

A physiological problem that sounds as though it would be unique to women but actually is not is breasts and the so-called difficulty in making a golf swing because of them. It's really almost a nonissue. Women with small or average-sized breasts will have no problems at all. Very large-breasted women may need to make some swing modifications; but for men with large, thick pectoral muscles, the problem is actually worse. The muscles are firmer and more "immovable" than breast tissue and can possibly get in the way more so than large breasts. Women with large breasts or men with large pectoral muscles may benefit from bending over more from the hips at address. This position will enable them to make a slightly more upright shoulder turn and allow the arms to swing over the breasts or chest muscles.

Golf Course Emergencies—Snakes

If you hit your ball near a snake that you think may be poisonous, don't play the ball. The Rules of Golf allow relief in this situation. The Rules of Golf are governed by three basic principles: (1) play the ball as it lies, (2) play the course as you find it, and (3) whenever the first two are not possible, do what is fair. Rule 1–4 of the Rules of Golf is entitled "Points Not Covered by the Rules" and deals with this situation: "If any point in dispute is not covered by the Rules, the decision shall be made in accordance with equity."

The U.S. Golf Association (USGA) publishes a book entitled *Decisions on the Rules of Golf* that covers unusual situations such as snakes and the rulings that have been made in accordance with the rules. A decision in a recent edition of the book discusses what should be done when a player's ball is near a snake—basically, don't play it. The ruling states: "In equity (Rule 1–4), the player should be permitted, without penalty, to drop a ball in the nearest spot not nearer the hole which is not dangerous." Common sense also tells us that you should leave the original ball for the snake and drop another one in a safer spot.

Ergo, you are entitled to drop your ball away from other dangerous situations, including bees' nests, nests of fire ants, and in the presence of other potentially dangerous animals.

If the ball is in a hazard, it should be dropped in a safe spot in the same hazard. If that's not possible, it should be dropped in a nearby hazard, but not nearer to the hole. If that's still not possible, the decision, unfortunately, then requires that the player may drop outside the hazard under penalty of one stroke. It is hoped that in friendly competitions at your club, this rather penal decision would be waived, and you would be allowed to drop outside the hazard and out of harm's way without further penalty.

Various regimens are used these days to treat poisonous snakebites. It's important to quickly move the victim to a place where he or she can get medical treatment.

If that's difficult or not possible, many treatments that have been recommended in the past should not be done. Specifically, don't try to suck out the venom. Cutting the leg and applying the mouth to the wound may secondarily infect the area. Very little venom is usually extracted, and the person sucking out the venom is at risk for ingesting some of it. A venom suction device is available that could be used if you have it as part of your emergency kit at the golf course.

Applying ice to the wound has been considered important in the past. However, it appears that ice may constrict blood supply to the area and cause further tissue death around the wound. Applying a tourniquet has been almost forbidden in the lay literature recently, but it may prevent any venom from reaching the central organs of the body. We often use tourniquets during surgery, and they can be applied safely by experienced personnel. They should not be applied tightly, should be released every fifteen minutes, and should not be left on for a total time of more than one hour except in a hospital situation.

What should be done? First, the player should rest, and the leg kept still to avoid spreading venom anywhere but locally. The player should be placed on a golf cart and transported without walking—this is one time I'm not advocating walking on a golf course. If this procedure is followed, most players can be returned to the clubhouse within minutes. They should be kept there, with the leg elevated to keep down swelling, until emergency medical personnel arrive to take the snakebite victim to the nearest emergency room.

The most important procedures to follow for snakebites in the United States are to stay calm, and remember that they're rarely fatal. North Carolina has the highest rate of poisonous snakebites per capita, but they usually only cause some local tissue damage except in the very young, the elderly, or infirm.

Golf Course Emergencies—Bee Stings

If you're not allergic to bee stings, a single sting may be painful and a nuisance, but it's really not a big deal.

An allergy to bee stings is a very big deal. It's also fairly common.

About 0.4 percent of the U.S. population is truly allergic to bee stings, meaning that they develop a serious, systemic reaction such as nausea, hives, or wheezing, rather than simply a localized swelling and pain. In the United States, bee stings account for forty to forty-five deaths annually, which is higher than that reported for any type of snakebite. Even if you aren't sure you are allergic, you should be suspicious if a family member is allergic to bee stings. The problem can also be inherited. About 15 percent of family members of a person allergic to bee stings will also be allergic.

All individuals allergic to bee stings should begin wearing a Medic Alert wrist bracelet that identifies this allergy. The bracelet can be obtained by writing Medic Alert Foundation, Turlock, California 95381, or by calling 1-800-432-5378.

Should you be stung by a bee, you risk a serious, potentially life-threatening reaction, including dangerously low blood pressure and swelling of your airway that could make it difficult to breathe. The emergency treatment for an allergic reaction to a bee sting "in the field" or on the golf course is an injection of epinephrine (adrenaline) under the skin. Kits are available in drugstores that contain the injection syringes and the drugs in the proper doses. Two available brands are Ana-Kit (Holister-Stier Laboratories) and Epi Pen (Center Laboratories). Get one of these kits and keep it in your golf bag and perhaps another in your car should you be stung away from the golf course.

Avoidance of the problem is also helpful. Keeping your ball out of the woods or weeds keeps you out of high-risk areas and is a good idea in general. If you see a potential beehive near your ball, don't go near it. The risk is not worth the loss of a two-dollar golf ball. If your playing partners object to your taking a drop away from this area, refer them to the *Decision Book on the Rules of Golf.* The decision I discussed earlier about dangerous snakes is analogous and allows you to drop away from the potentially dangerous beehive.

Lyme Disease

Until the late 1970s, the only golf problem associated with limes was an overaccumulation of them in the gin-and-tonic glass at the nineteenth hole. Then along came Lyme disease, a relatively recently discovered disease. Its name comes from an outbreak of the disease first reported in 1975 near Lyme, Connecticut.

Lyme disease is caused by the bite of a deer tick. The tick transmits the organism, the spirochete *Borrelia burgdorferi,* that then causes the disease.

The symptoms of the disease initially include fatigue, headache, fever, and joint and muscle aches. Characteristic of the disease is a red, ring-shaped rash at the site of a tick bite. In its full-blown state, the disease can mimic severe neurologic problems such as multiple sclerosis, and it can also cause joint damage similar to that done by rheumatoid arthritis.

Golfers risk being bitten by a tick when walking in heavily wooded areas or areas of long grass. Therefore, the best measure to take when playing golf is never to miss a fairway or green! Studies have shown that the golfers who have the highest risk to diseases from ticks are high handicappers because they are often in the woods. Women also do not develop tick-related problems as often. The one medical study mentioning this fact noted that women were in the woods less, and if they were, they didn't look as long for their ball.

If you stray from the short grass, however, check for ticks on your skin and just under your hairline. If a tick is quickly removed, the chance of its transmitting the disease is very small. Checking your skin carefully after coming out of the woods is especially important in the summer or early autumn, when the tick population is at its highest.

If you think you have been exposed to a significant tick bite recently and if you develop a sudden onset of fever, rash, headache or other neurologic problems, or joint aches, you should see a doctor as soon as possible. Lyme disease is almost never fatal, but a similar disease caused by a tick bite, Rocky Mountain spotted fever, can be fatal if not treated. Both diseases respond well if treated early with antibiotics, but you need to see your doctor to accurately diagnose the diseases.

Eye Problems—Glasses, Sunglasses, Adjustments, Rain

Eye problems affect golfers just as they affect all individuals. But there are some special problems associated with golf. First, if you play a lot in the midday sun, should you wear sunglasses to protect your eyes?

Absolutely. Sunlight consists of certain radiation bands of ultraviolet light that have been shown to cause cataracts if one is exposed to them for long periods. More and more professional golfers are now wearing sunglasses.

I suspect the reason that sunglasses were not used frequently in the past is that they obscure shadows somewhat. Professional golfers need to see shadows well to read the greens in many cases (that's why on overcast days, greens are harder to read). The grain and the slope of the green change shade when viewed from various angles, and these subtleties may not be well appreciated in sunglasses. In addition, seeing the pin can be a bit more difficult with sunglasses.

Glasses are now available, however, that are clear, don't obscure shadows or decrease visual acuity, yet block ultraviolet rays. If you're going to start wearing sunglasses to play golf, check with your optometrist, and get these newer lenses that won't cause problems reading greens.

Many older golfers are now moving into the bifocal stages. The standard bifocal lens has one power lens on the lower border of the glass frame and another power lens on the upper border of the glass frame. If you are playing golf in bifocals, you may benefit from adjusting this. Most of the time, you look out of the lower lens to read and the upper lens for viewing distant objects.

The problem is that reading lenses are set up to focus at about thirteen to seventeen inches away. The ball is about four to six feet away from your eyes, and the standard bifocal forces one to view the ball through this lens. Thus, the ball will be blurry to you and can be very disconcerting. You can also discuss this problem with your optometrist, but the standard setup for the lenses is not mandatory. You can adjust the setup because some golfers have difficulty focusing on the ball through their bifocals. Another solution is progressive lenses with varying focal lengths, which will help you find a viewing angle that brings the ball and also distant objects into focus.

Senior Golfers

The PGA Senior Tour is virtually an experiment in seeing how well senior golfers respond to the stress of playing frequent golf under competitive situations. Obviously, the senior players have more health problems than their younger counterparts. They have coped nicely.

Many of the problems of senior players are described in the various chapters of the book. As with all golfers, the most common problems to the seniors occur in the back and the elbows.

Back problems are almost endemic among the senior players. Given the twisting and turning required by the golf swing and the necessity to hit thousands of practice balls to get to the Senior PGA Tour, it's easy to see why players could develop back problems. Many of the players used chiropractic manipulation for back and neck problems and seemed happy with the results.

Because of the frequent back and elbow problems on the Senior Tour, practice patterns are different. The seniors don't hit as many balls as the players on the Junior Tour. It's a major strain on the back, and the years of playing have grooved their swings enough that long practice sessions are not as necessary.

Dave Hill has commented about the lighter practice patterns, "Hell, we don't need to practice as much. My swing's a hell of a lot more grooved than those young whippersnappers. Mostly, we work on our putting and short game—that's where the money is out here."

Walt Zembriski has said that he thought everybody out there (on the PGA Senior Tour) has had problems with tennis elbow at one time or another. Among the players with elbow problems, various treatments were used. Some used a tennis elbow brace under the elbow to transfer the force off the elbow to further down the forearm. Dave Hill said this was popular for a while: "It used to be everybody was wearing the thing, but you don't see as many of them anymore." Surgery for the problem is definitely the exception because most players are able to play through the problems.

The senior players are helped by the trailer that follows them from tour site to tour site, a situation that also occurs for the PGA Tour and LPGA Tour. The trailer contains some lightweight equipment as well as exercise bicycles and is always staffed by two physical therapists. Bill Dolan, one of the physical therapists who has been in the Senior Tour trailer, talked about his role: "We try to help the players with their aerobic fitness mainly, as many of them ride golf carts and get almost no other aerobic exercise. Also we've tried to stress preventive measures like stretching and staying flexible. A few of the players come in and use the weights available, but not too many."

Virtually all the players use the trailer to some degree. A few, like Bruce Crampton, and of course, Gary Player, use it often, visiting almost every day. Others vary in their routine, but many ride exercise bikes in the trailer for some aerobic fitness.

The average player can learn several lessons from the seniors. First, they all work to keep their weight down. Excess weight puts a lot of extra stress on bad backs or arthritic hips, knees, or ankles. Second, most do some exercise in addition to their golf to allow them to maintain their conditioning and control their weight. Third, practicing too much as you age is difficult on the body and may not be as necessary. However, a good preround warm-up is still essential to help you get off to a good start and avoid injuries. Fourth, the pros with physical ailments have all made swing adjustments to take stress off their problem areas.

You and Your Golf Cart

My dislike for golf carts has been well documented in other sections of this book. Golf carts do a lot of bad things for the game of golf—they prevent golfers from deriving any exercise benefit from playing, they slow play, they require courses to build unsightly golf paths, and they damage turf in multiple places where the carts go off the paths. What good do they do? Well, they make a lot of money for golf professionals and for golf courses, so they're here to stay. I'm not so naive to believe that my diatribes will end the blight that is golf carts on U.S. golf courses.

I know individuals will continue to use golf carts and, unfortunately, probably in greater and greater numbers. So I think it's important to talk for a few minutes about using them safely. As Norm Abram always says on that PBS television show about wood-working, "Be sure to use, understand, and follow all the instructions that come with your power tools." A golf cart is a major-league power tool, not unlike a car, and should be used safely and with caution at all times.

Unlike cars, golf carts don't come with structurally safe roofs or roll bars to prevent injuries to the passengers.

Golf cars can turn over and have done so. You may be familiar with a golfer named Dennis Walters, a paraplegic who gives shows and exhibitions about playing golf with that disability. Dennis was a promising amateur from New Jersey in the early 1970s until he tipped over in a golf cart and was paralyzed.

Be very careful on downslopes or sideslopes. These places are the most dangerous to drive a cart, and you should always try to stay on the cart path in these situations if at all possible. Remember, cars on the road are not usually driven over grass, which is quite slick and gives much less traction than do tires on the road. You need to be careful on wet days or on wet grass. Never "hot rod" and see how fast you can drive the cart. You may not get the chance to do that again.

Please keep your legs inside the golf cart at all times. Recently, I had to do a major knee ligament reconstruction on a good friend of mine. An avid golfer, he was playing in a cart when his foot caught the edge of a retaining fence and twisted his leg behind him. Almost every ligament in his knee was torn. While I appreciate the business, I can assure you that most orthopaedic surgeons are quite busy, and we emphasize the importance of preventing injuries such as this.

Playing with Disabilities

Golf is a wonderful sport in that it can be played by individuals of all ages, and almost no health problem should disqualify somebody from enjoying a game they love. Amputees, stroke victims, and individuals with paralyzing nerve damage all can continue to play golf and should be encouraged to do so.

Amputees can easily play golf. There is even an organization called the National Amputee Golf Association (P.O. Box 1228, Amherst, NH 03031 1-603-673-1135) that sponsors golf tournaments and encourages amputees to continue playing golf. Most of the amputees have had lower extremity amputations. Somebody who has suffered this problem and wishes to play golf can do so with few problems.

If golf is a major enjoyment in your life, after an amputation you should be encouraged to continue with it. One adjustment that you may wish to make is to ask your prosthetist to design a different ankle mechanism for you. Most prostheses have solid ankle mechanisms with only a cushioned heel that allows some compression at the heel during walking to simulate ankle motion. However, single-axis and rotating hinge ankle joints are available. Golfers will do better with these type ankles and may want to request them in their prosthesis. They are heavier and more expensive than a standard ankle in a prosthesis. In addition, they may be less stable and wear out slightly more quickly. Still, if you wish to play golf with a prosthesis, you'll benefit from one of these movable ankles.

Upper extremity amputees are much rarer, but golf is still possible. Special prosthetic attachments that allow the amputee to grip the club can be designed. Simply ask your prosthetist, and they will help you. Even bilateral upper extremity amputees have been known to continue playing golf.

Being paralyzed from the waist down (paraplegia) either from an injury or from a stroke doesn't mean you have to give up golf, although it may be difficult. Conversely, not all paraplegics will be able to play golf. You need to have the ability to walk with support (crutches) and have some balance remaining. If you have this ability and wish to continue playing golf, there are special crutches available for golfers that will help support you during a golf swing. The National Rehabilitation Hospital in Arlington, Virginia, produces and sells such crutches. The golfer uses these special supports with one arm and then swings one-handed. The crutches are designed with pods on the ends to cause minimal, if any, damage to the golf course.

Earlier, we mentioned Dennis Walters who is unable to walk. Dennis plays with the use of a special golf cart and swings from a rotating seat. This setup is still a possibility for golfers who have lost the use of their lower limbs from paralysis or strokes. It is, however, much more expensive.

The president of the National Rehabilitation Hospital, Edward Eschenbach, is paralyzed from the midwaist but continues to play golf using these specially designed crutches. Ed hits a golf ball more than 200 yards and shoots in the eighties. He's a real inspiration to watch. So don't give up hope!

11

Playing in Difficult Conditions

Playing golf in very hot weather, especially in the Deep South in the summer, can be dangerous if you're not careful and don't take the necessary precautions. Over-heating is not a trifling matter—the old bromides from the Southern football coaches about its making you "a man" and not drinking during hot weather to "get you in shape" can be extremely dangerous if heeded. Heat production may be increased tenfold to twentyfold by strenuous exertion, and it should be remembered that heat stroke is third only to head and spinal cord injuries and heart failure as a cause of death among American athletes.

Preparation begins with the proper dress. Light-colored clothes don't absorb the sun's rays and will keep you cooler. All-cotton fabrics also are less sticky and breathe better in hot, humid conditions. You cool off in hot weather by sweating, but clothing restricts the evaporation of sweat and makes sweating much less efficient. Therefore, I'd also recommend shorts at all times in very hot weather (except for diabetics, who

*Figure 11–1
A golfer
prepared
to play in
the warm
weather—
white cotton
shirt, wide-
brimmed hat,
and sunglasses.
Shorts may
also help when
it's really hot.*

Courtesy Jim Moriarty/
Mr. Ed Ibarguen

probably should avoid extremely hot conditions and should always keeps their legs covered while playing).

A wide-brimmed hat will help a great deal because a lot of body heat is released through the head (see Figure 11–1). You may even wish to wear one of the safari-type hats, which Ivan Lendl used on the pro tennis tour on very hot days. This type will keep your head and neck areas well-shaded. Sunglasses also are a good idea. Triathletes and marathoners are now using these routinely, because the eyes use a lot of energy on bright, sun-lit days.

Two towels with your golf bag are a big help. One should be kept moist at all times to wipe off perspiration, clean your grips, and keep you a bit cooler. The other towel should be dry to allow your hands and grips to stay dry for a better grip during your swing. Tennis sweatbands may also help. When I played in very hot weather, I used tennis sweatbands and would soak them in water at various times. They keep your hands cool and dry, helping you grip the club better.

You need to drink a lot while playing. Bringing a plastic water bottle with some fluid is very helpful if your course doesn't have a lot of fountains. Remember to drink before you go out to play as well. By the time you get thirsty, you could already be severely dehydrated. Nobody ever drinks enough in hot weather. Typically, we replace only about 70 percent of the fluid we lose by sweating during vigorous activity, even when we are trying to drink a lot of fluid during the activity. In hot climates, physical exercise can cause us to lose one to two liters (about one-fourth to one-half a gallon) of sweat per hour.

What should you drink? A shaker full of martinis is not recommended. Consuming alcohol is very dangerous in hot weather. If you have a few drinks in the nineteenth hole on a very hot day, the safest thing to do is not to play that day—or make sure you have them after you play. Oddly, another dangerous drink can be diet cola. It has some additives that actually act to make you lose additional fluid when it's hot and you're sweating.

Pure water is probably the best all-around drink. There are special athletic drinks that replace the electrolytes you lose when you sweat, but you need to be careful that they aren't loaded with sugar, which can slow absorption in the stomach. Most of the available "athletic-type" drinks have a high sugar content. If you are going to bring them with you, they probably should be diluted with some water. The advantage these drinks have is that they often are tastier than water, and you may drink more of them than pure water.

We've heard for years that salt tablets are a necessity in hot weather and should be used because, by sweating, you are losing salt. The truth is that salt tablets are not only unnecessary, but also possibly dangerous except in unusual circumstances. When you sweat, the salt content you lose is fairly low—your body hoards salt at all costs. You really need to replace the water you lose more than the salt. By drinking an electrolyte-replacement drink, you definitely don't need salt tablets. Lightly salting your food the day before or the morning of play is probably enough. If you have high blood pressure, however, you need to discuss salt loss with your internist, because salting your food can exacerbate the problem.

Golfers with significant health problems, especially heart disease, need to be very careful in hot weather. It may be wiser not to play when the thermometer gets way up there. I'd certainly advise you to check with your doctor or cardiologist if you have these problems. If you're taking medications, these can make you more susceptible to the heat, and I'd again check with your doctor. Medications that are definitely dangerous in hot weather include antidepressants, antihistamines (including over-the-counter medicines such as Benadryl and Tavist-D), and many heart medications, especially the class known as beta-blockers.

Finally, although I've expressed my reservations about using golf carts many times, the only good time to use one may be in very hot weather, especially if you have any health problems at all.

What happens if you or one of your playing partners appears to succumb to the heat? This situation is potentially life-threatening and should be considered as such. The most important treatment rule is to cool off that person. Get the player out of the sun—into the clubhouse if possible or into the shade of the woods if not. Remove as much clothing as is reasonable, and start placing cool, wet towels over the body. Somebody else in the group should also be contacting the clubhouse or golf shop to make plans to get the person off the course and to a hospital emergency room as quickly as possible.

Cold weather isn't as dangerous as hot weather, and in golf it does not usually pose significant health risks. The reason is that golf is almost never played in weather cold enough to cause problems like frostbite or hypothermia. If you play in temperatures that cold, a visit to a psychiatrist may be the best remedy. The most important rule to remember when you play in cold weather is simply to dress carefully in multiple layers of clothing. This will keep you warm much more efficiently than a single, very thick and heavy jacket or sweater. Again, alcohol should be avoided when it's cold because it restricts blood flow to the hands and feet and conceivably could result in some damage to those areas.

One other helpful item on very cold days is a hand warmer. In competition, be careful not to carry the hand warmer near your golf balls. The device will heat the golf balls, which technically is illegal.

The Sun and Your Skin

The sun's rays damage the skin. Getting a tan may look healthy, but most sun lovers, including golfers who don't protect themselves properly, are simply putting themselves at risk of skin cancer. Sunlight contains ultraviolet (UV) light that can have deleterious effects on the skin. These ultraviolet rays are of two types: UV-A, which causes tanning; and UV-B, which burns the skin and damages it.

Wearing a hat, especially one with a wide brim, will help a little. Clothing is also helpful in preventing sunburn and skin damage. Unfortunately, clothing will not block all the sun's rays. And white cotton, like many golf shirts, lets through a significant portion of the sun's rays. Unfortunately, as I said earlier, white cotton is also the coolest material you can wear on hot days, so this situation is a Catch-22.

To truly prevent damage to the skin, sunscreen protection is a must. The books say that you should use a sunscreen with an SPF (sun protection factor) of fifteen. But it's a bit more complicated than that.

Let's look at what the SPF means. It means, basically, the amount of time you can spend in the sun to get the same effect on your skin as one hour in the sun without protection. Thus, an SPF of fifteen should allow you to stay in the sun for fifteen hours relatively safely. In addition, all sunscreens block UV-B rays, and the SPF specifically refers to the blocking of these rays. But not all sunscreens block UV-A rays, which are less dangerous but also can cause some long-term damage. Still, it's a good idea to choose a sunscreen that blocks both sets of rays, and that should be listed on the squeeze bottle or tube.

However, the SPF is designed in a laboratory. Also, it's measured by the use of one ounce of the sunscreen. Most people rarely use more than one-tenth of an ounce at any one time. In addition, not all sunscreens are waterproof, and they last a variable amount of time. Theoretically, they should be reapplied every two hours, but this is rarely done.

Another factor to consider is your skin type. I am fairly dark and swarthy, and I tan easily, and I never had a sunburn while playing golf. My skin is relatively protected from the harmful effects of the sun. Hispanics, African Americans, and Latins are protected even more. But fair-skinned blondes or redheads need to be especially careful. If you fall into this category, protecting your skin is a must.

Dermatologists currently recommend much higher sunscreen protection than SPF fifteen. Try to use one at least as high as thirty or forty if possible, especially if you are fair-skinned. This SPF likely will provide adequate protection even if you don't apply it thickly enough, sweat it off quickly, and don't reapply it while playing. If you wish to reapply it, getting it on your hands while playing can be messy and can ruin your grip on the club. Stick roll-ons are available if you truly wish to be careful and reapply the sunscreen while playing.

Always apply the sunscreen generously and at least thirty to sixty minutes before going out to play, because it works better if it has soaked in. Remember to apply it on cloudy days as well. Weather can change, and ultraviolet rays get through the clouds to some extent. Don't forget the sides of the neck and the "V" of the chest—lots of damage can occur there. Applying the sunscreen to the arms is also important—if you use a very high SPF, you don't have to wear long sleeves.

If you have a problem with stinging in your eyes, either don't apply the sunscreen to your forehead (but then wear a hat all the time!) or be sure you're washing your hands well after you've applied the lotion so you aren't rubbing your eyes with your fingers. Another option is to apply the sunscreen high on your forehead, and wear a sweatband just above your eyes. This will cover the skin in that area and also prevent the sunscreen from getting into your eyes. I'll mention a little bit about using sunglasses and other eye protection in the section that deals with your eyes.

A good way to avoid overexposure to the sun's rays is to avoid sand traps and water hazards. Many of you know that it's possible to get a good tan while skiing. The reason is that snow reflects almost 90% of the sun's rays. Similarly, sand traps reflect about 20% of those rays, while water hazards reflect about 10% in the morning and late afternoon but almost 100% at noon. Grass only reflects about 2% of them, so keep it in the fairway—if only we all could!

Using hats, visors, and sunscreens is similar to getting used to wearing a seatbelt—it may seem foreign at first, but soon it feels strange not to use them. And your skin will be a lot safer for it.

Playing in the Rain and the Wind

Playing in the rain is rarely a health hazard. It's more of a nuisance. But there are some things you can do to make it easier. Obviously, you should have an umbrella. Keep a towel dry by placing one through the staves of the umbrella underneath it. Now you have one towel that always stays dry and allows you to use it to keep your hands dry.

Keeping your clubs' grips dry is imperative in wet weather. Most good golf bags have bag covers or other rain covers that should be kept over the bag to keep water from draining into the bag and soaking the grips. Most grips still get wet in the rain. The dry towel under your umbrella can be used to dry them.

Playing in the rain with a wet golf glove feels miserable. Not only is it not as effective as a dry golf glove, but also probably less effective than no glove at all. I used golf gloves until 1971, when I was playing in the New England Amateur in Rutland, Vermont. On the last day we had to play thirty-six holes, and it rained all day. After twenty-seven holes, all my gloves were soaking wet, so I elected to play the last nine without one. I shot a thirty-one on that nine and never used a golf glove after that day.

If you use a golf glove, you need to keep it dry. That's rarely possible for the entire eighteen holes, so you'll need several available. Again, the best place to put the glove you're using to keep it dry between shots is on the staves of your umbrella. Other gloves should be kept in your golf bag.

Use golf shoes with good, long spikes. Keep them clean when playing in the rain. Wet grass accumulates around the spikes on wet days and makes them less effective. Poor footing can be dangerous in wet weather and could cause a serious injury if you slip and fall. Spikeless shoes are becoming the rage these days. They are becoming mandatory on more and more courses around the country, and indeed there's some evidence that they keep the putting surfaces smoother. Certainly, their use eliminates spike marks. But one often-heard complaint is that a player can slip while using them in wet weather, especially on slopes. So be very careful in those conditions.

If it's cool and raining, it's possible to get very cold on the course. Again, multiple layers of light clothing will help protect you. The outer layer should be a waterproof and preferably windproof type of light jacket.

Playing in the wind will affect your score, but it has minimal affect on your health. The only important thing to remember is that the wind can dry out your skin and give you a windburn similar to a sunburn. If it's a sunny, windy day, you could incur a significant amount of sun damage to your skin. As described earlier, sunscreens are even more important in windy and sunny conditions.

Lightning and Dangerous Weather

The most dangerous situation a golfer can face on the course is lightning. Lightning kills. Thirty percent of people struck by lightning are killed by it, and 70 percent are severely injured in some way. Thus, the best treatment is prevention.

As I mentioned in chapter 2, in 1975 at the Western Open at Butler National Golf Course near Chicago, lightning enveloped the course, and officials considered themselves lucky that numerous spectators were not killed. Three professionals—Lee Trevino, Bobby Nichols, and Jerry Heard—were struck indirectly by lightning flashes, and all but Heard were hospitalized. Fortunately, none of the injuries were life-threatening. In 1991 at the U.S. Open at Hazeltine near Minneapolis, a spectator was killed by lightning. Later that same year, another spectator was killed by lightning during the PGA Championship at Crooked Stick Golf Club near Indianapolis.

In a thirty-four-year period ending in 1974, the National Climatic Data Service reported that there were more than seven thousand lightning fatalities in the United States, or about two hundred per year. Of these, more than six hundred occurred on golf courses, or about eighteen per year. Lightning kills more people in the United States than any other natural disaster. The worst states for lightning injuries on golf courses are Florida and North Carolina.

The Rules of Golf are very specific regarding lightning. They allow any player who feels threatened by nearby lightning to suspend play. During a formal competition, the committee in charge should suspend play whenever thunder and lightning are nearby. However, even before that time, the player may stop playing if he feels threatened.

Once play is suspended, the Rules of Golf allow you to finish out the hole you are playing. Rule 6-8 reads: "If they are in the process of playing a hole, they may continue provided they do so without delay."

Do not pay attention to this rule! It absolutely should be changed! When play is suspended, stop playing immediately. Remember that a thunderstorm can travel at fifty miles an hour. Finishing that par five in twelve minutes can allow the thunderstorm to travel ten miles and put you at severe risk. Finishing any hole is simply not worth it when lightning is nearby. Getting in that extra shot or putt could cost you your life!

The best time to stop playing is not when you see lightning but when you hear thunder. Forget the rules about counting the time between the lightning flash and the thunderclap. Thunder is caused by lightning. If you hear thunder and don't see lightning, that doesn't mean there isn't a problem. Don't say, "I don't see any lightning, let's keep playing." Seventy-five percent of lightning goes from cloud to cloud rather than from cloud to ground. So if you wait to see a lightning flash, you'll miss three-quarters of them.

If you see lightning or hear thunder, get off the course immediately. Get to the clubhouse or a nearby maintenance building. If that's not possible, look for some nearby homes. Ask to seek shelter there or at least in the person's garage, and hope the homeowner will be understanding.

If you can't get off the course, drop your clubs, and get as far away from them as possible. There are often some small shelters on the course. If so, seek them out. Get in the center of the shelter, take off your golf spikes, get away from any golf clubs or umbrellas—leave them outside the shelter—and avoid any other metal objects. Preferably, stand in the middle of the shelter, and don't lean on anything because it may conduct electricity if lightning strikes.

If no building or shelter is available, get as deep as possible into a forested area and look for a low-lying area. Avoid single trees or an isolated group of trees. Also, stay as far away as possible from power lines if they are nearby. If no heavily forested area is nearby and you are basically stuck, seek the lowest ground possible in a fairway, avoiding all metal such as pipes, sprinkler heads, or golf carts.

Once in this low-lying area, crouch as low as possible, staying on the balls of your feet if possible. This position is better than lying down, because if lightning strikes in the area, there is less of your body in contact with the ground to conduct the electricity. Foursomes or groups should spread out so that lightning does not flash from member to member. Also, stay far away from bodies of water, which are great conductors of electricity. Being close to water is the least desirable situation, and it should never happen if you plan properly and get off the course as soon as possible after you suspect there may be lightning in the area.

If a group member is struck by lightning, several very dangerous things can occur. First, the person could be killed almost instantly. The cause of death is usually a cardiopulmonary arrest, because electricity changes the electrical pattern of the heart and can cause it either to stop beating or to beat erratically. However, the victim still may be revived if nearby golfers know cardiopulmonary resuscitation (CPR) and begin it immediately. One group member must inform the clubhouse as quickly as possible because the treatment in this instance is not only to start CPR, but also to get the victim to the hospital as fast as possible.

If a lightning victim is alive, burns become another concern. In this case, clothing may be burned—remove it immediately and quickly get cold, wet towels on the burned areas. Golf bag towels can be dipped in a nearby stream and used.

Lightning also may cause seizures by changing the electrical activity of the brain. Little can be done for this except to keep the victim from injuring himself or herself during the seizure. Try to protect the victim's head, preventing it from hitting any hard objects. Do not place your hands in the victim's mouth—they will not swallow their tongue.

There are several myths concerning lightning. One is that a lightning victim remains electrified and should not be touched. This is incorrect and has led to unnecessary deaths because attempts at resuscitation were delayed. Another is "Lightning never strikes the same place twice." That's wrong. Lightning often strikes the same place twice. So don't think you're home free after the first bolt hits nearby.

Basically, prevention is the best cure. Don't allow a lightning disaster to happen—get off the course at the first sign of potential thunderstorms. It may interrupt or cancel the best round of your life, but that's a lot better than having the score engraved on your tombstone.

The upshot of this entire book is that whether the problems come from the sky or from within your own body, you can deal with them by using knowledge, common sense, and in most cases, some effort. Injuries can be prevented. And if you have incapacities, there's seldom if ever a case in which you can't overcome them or play around them and continue to enjoy this game of a lifetime, the greatest game of all.

Index